FINANCIAL TIPS TO HELP KIDS

PROVEN METHODS FOR TEACHING KIDS MONEY
MANAGEMENT AND FINANCIAL RESPONSIBILITY

BUKKY EKINE-OGUNLANA

CONTENTS

Introduction   9

1. Finance For Kids   13
2. Teaching Kids Financial Management   27
3. Learn To Say No   42
4. Money And Kids   48
5. Savings   58
6. Building A spending Plan   65
7. Ways To Teach Kids About Money   72
8. Young Kids And Money   86
9. Financial Tips For Kids   116
10. How To Be Successful Children   125
11. What Your Kids Should Know   134
12. How To Raise Kids Succeesfully   139
13. Introduction To Entrepreneurship   146

Conclusion   157
The Book   159
Other Books You'll Love!   161
References   167

© **Copyright Bukky Ekine-Ogunlana 2020 – All rights reserved.**

The content contained within this book may not be reproduced, duplicated or transmitted without direct written permission from the author or the publisher.

Under no circumstance will any blame or legal responsibility be held against the publisher, or author, for any damages, reparation, or monetary loss due to the information contained within this book. Either directly or indirectly. You are responsible for your own choices, actions and results.

Legal Notice:

This book is copyright protected. This book is only for personal use. You cannot amend, distribute, sell, use, quote or paraphrase any part, or the content within this book, without the consent of the author or publisher.

Disclaimer Notice:

Please note the information contained within this document is for educational and entertainment purpose only. All effort has been executed to present accurate, up to date, and reliable, complete information. No warranties of any kind are declared or implied. Readers acknowledge that the author is not engaging in the rendering of legal, financial, medical or professional advice. The content within this book has been derived from various sources. Please consult a licensed professional before attempting any techniques outlined in this book

By reading this document , the reader agrees that under no circumstances is the author responsible for any losses, direct or indirect, which are incurred as a result of the use of the information contained within this document, Including, but not limited to,—errors, omissions, or inaccuracies.

Published by

TCEC Publishing

TCEC House

14-18 Ada Street, London Fields,

E8 4QU, England, Great Britain.

DEDICATION

This book is dedicated to our three amazing children and all the wonderful children all over the world who over the years have passed through the T.C.E.C 6-16 year's programme. Thank you for the opportunity to serve you and invest in your colourful and bright future.

INTRODUCTION

It's a universal search, don't we all agree, the search for money. It's part of why we are on a job, isn't it? We work to earn money, not just money in itself, but for what money can procure for us.

As a means of exchange, even from ancient times, money has always been one of the most elusive things the world over. Most people are in endless search for money. Grab some, and you see the need to seek more, then more, and more of money to exchange for the increasing material things we require in modern time to lead a comfortable life.

It is however increasingly becoming the case that the problem with most people isn't the complete lack of money or insufficient fund, but the mismanagement or abuse of money. And the result is never pleasant for anyone.

Generation after generation, we have seen mistakes and errors repeated regarding how people treat money, leaving the vast majority of people poor, impoverished, deprived and destitute.

I'd like to see a change.

Don't you?

My kids have got to make a difference after I've taught them how to relate with money. I believe the desire for most parents is mutual. We should all be teaching our kids about money. And starting early is key. We don't want them making grievous mistakes or setting off in life knowing nothing about how to grow finances, or treating money with disrespect.

I needed to be certain that parents have the right knowledge with which to equip their children from early in life with viable and sustainable financial tips. It's a very important responsibility kids can learn. They need to know how to account for and manage money.

Oh! Have we heard and seen examples of kids who do not understand the concept of money management or how to handle money to impact their quality of life? It's important for adults to teach kids these lessons which can positively impact the rest of their lives.

After reading this guide, please feel free to leave a review based on your findings and how useful the guide was to you. It is always important to hear feedback, so please feel free to leave a helpful review and if you feel like it warrants it, recommend the guide to your friends and family.

1

FINANCE FOR KIDS

It's never too soon to start teaching children about finances. It can be hard to talk to kids about money. You may have to acknowledge your own mistakes, and potentially even inject a sense of reality into your wide-eyed offspring. And the economic situation of society today continues to worsen, with the gap between the rich and the poor getting wider, it is more important nowadays than ever before to teach the importance of managing your finances, as early as possible.

DAN'S MUM'S APPROACH

Dan walked up to his mum and requested for £5 for materials for his school project. She knew how important the project was for him and that he needed to get a good grade, but she also needed to make him understand the value of money. So she started by asking him, "What can you do to earn this money you are asking from me?"

Amazed that such question could come from his mum, Dan said: "Mum, seriously? Can't I just have it?"

His mother replied, "You need to know the difference between earning something and getting it on a platter."

Dan was rapt in attention now. He did not only show affirmation but respect for his mum. In engaging with his mother and getting a clear, firm answer, he was able to gain a clearer insight into what the real world is like - where you need to work for the things you want, and the things you don't necessarily even want but need to survive.

"When you work to get something done," the mum continues, "how will you handle it?"

Dan replied "Of course, I'll handle it well, mum. I won't allow any scratch on it."

"Do you know how important it is to do a good job?" she asked.

"Yes, otherwise you won't get repeat business." Dan quipped.

His mum proudly answered, "You're learning, good."

"When I return from school today, I'll help pick up your items from the grocery store," Dan offers.

"Now, you earn it with respect," she told him and gave him a loving hug as she tucked the £5.00 in his hands.

That was all she did to infuse in Dan the understanding of the value of money and how to handle it.

TALKING ABOUT MONEY

Talking to your children about money is important [1]. It's difficult to know when to have the 'money talk' with your children, as all parents are difficult. The first real talk about work and money should happen long before your child has their first bank account, or at least before they are aware of what a bank account even is. That way, you establish the idea that you only spend money that you have earned. This helps to inculcate a sense of fiscal responsibility in your child. Turn everyday's activities into teaching moments. When you go shopping, talk about comparing prices, looking for good deals, and how prices go up and down. If you drop by the cash machine, explain that you have to fund your bank account in order to take money out of the cash machine. When you pay your bills, talk about how debit/credit cards work, and about debt and interest. As your children get older, talk about the importance of insurance, and its costs.

If you are having an especially difficult time getting the conversation started, consider online resources, alongside thorough use of this guide, taking the information that works for you and utilising it alongside other materials and online tools. In society, we're often taught about the 'taking' side of finances but not so much about the significance of giving back. Get your children involved in the process of donating to charity would therefore likely be a wise thing to do. Allow them to choose who they give to out of their own conviction, and doing so willingly, sacrificially and joyfully. Not only does this give them a sense of importance and new-found confidence, it allows them to research charities and find one that means something to them.

Encouraging children to work is also a crucial aspect of your child building a solid framework of their personal finances. Working can teach your child valuable life's lessons. Even if your kid is too young to work, set up an allowance system in which they have to complete certain tasks in order to receive rewards. Create a budget for the things you provide. Make categories such as clothing and electronics, and allow them to decide whether to spend or save for higher quality items. Set up a checking and *savings* account, and reward them for saving.

When your child gets their first full time job, you should then begin to teach them about basic investment plans. It's never too soon to start saving and investing; and it will help them to learn how to slice up their pay cheque. Teach them about how to make the most of their account package.

THINGS TO AVOID

There are a few things you should avoid doing. Don't allow yourself become the only financial lifeline for your children, young or as adults [2]. If your child overdrafts or overspends, make sure they learn from their mistakes while undergoing little or no harm. If they are damaging their credit, however, you may want to step in and help them out. Don't set their financial goals for them. Let them determine their own goals. It's the only way they'll learn to stay financially disciplined.

In short, the sooner you start teaching your children how to be fiscally responsible the more likely it will become a part of how they manage their finances. Continue to advise them on their finances as they take up a job and begin to think about savings and investment. Yet, don't exert too much control over their decisions; remain an adviser, not a manupulator. We are to go all the way through this journey with our kids and are to get them through the more difficult aspects of it.

Pete had a son who had just got his first job, and though he didn't need it, Pete requested that his son pay him 25% of his wages. He explained how this would be what he would pay in rent if he were to be earning his money in the real-world, where bills and rent are commonplace. In doing so, Pete ensured that he didn't become a financial lifeline to his son, as he now knew the value of money and knew more about budgeting than he would ever have done otherwise. Pete did put this money into a trust for his son, so everybody was a winner.

LET THEM DECIDE

Now that you have begun the process, and are working to change the model your kids have lived by, get rid of allowances; determine the appropriate amount for them to manage, and help them work out a spending plan. You need to let them manage what's available to them. This is key to their success. If you continue to intervene when you think, or even know, they are making a mistake, they would have a diminished opportunity to learn.

You will need to take a position of an adviser and counsellor. What I mean is, it is okay for you to give them advice on a spending decision, and it is perfectly acceptable to try to help them work through all the benefits and detriments to a decision. The hard part is leaving the final decision to them.

Of course, there will be times you may have to step in and say enough is enough, or I am sorry, but you can't do that because X, Y or Z.

I know of a couple whose child had made some very questionable decisions regarding the spending of her money. Rather than taking care of the mobile/cellphone bill, car insurance and maintenance, school expenses, and other agreed responsibilities, this child chose to spend virtually all of her money on clothes, App Store downloads, entertainment, and eating out. When the parents terminated the mobile phone contract and confiscated the car keys from her because it was uninsured, their child couldn't understand why, and thought her parents were being so unreasonable.

As parents, it's obviously very difficult to tell your child something they don't want to hear - especially if it's something you don't want to even acknowledge yourself. But, think "Enough is enough." Intervene when the mistake isn't going to be learnt from otherwise, as the consequences otherwise may be critical.

In time, the child did realise her mistakes and now has a much healthier relationship with money, now prioritising the importance of keeping her car on the road and having a working phone, over clothes she doesn't really need.

I believe the parents did the right thing in this case.

First, there was the basic responsibility of the child paying for the benefit of the mobile/cellphone use. It would have been a different situation if the parents had agreed to pay the phone bill; but that was not the agreed conditions. The second, and more important responsibility, was the uninsured driver and responsibility to others. If this teen had caused an accident while the car was not insured, the injured persons and their damaged property would not be indemnified, being with no insurance cover. Then the parents would have had to pay for the injuries and damages.

With most children, once they realise there is a limited supply of income and they are in control of where it goes, they begin to get very interested in prioritising the things they want to spend their money on and getting the best deal they can. This is where they begin to learn the difference between "cheap" and a "goodbuy". Help them discern when a good deal really is a good deal, versus a "cheap" but bad deal.

A VITAL QUESTION

Help your child to stay focused on the spending plan they set up. Teach them to ask the question advertisers don't want asked: "Is it in my spending plan?" Asking this question alone is a very powerful tool for bringing control and checks to spending. It tends to force you to think about why you are buying an item. In other words, is it a priority? If it is not, don't buy it. Save your money for something of greater value to you [3]. Kids must know how not to spend money on things they can do without.

Watch how your child responds to that question. Yet, if it's not in their spending plan, it's still OK if they go ahead and make the purchase, as long as they have figured out how to adjust the spending plan to include it, and as long as they have not compromised their obligations to other categories for which they have responsibilities. If they buy it and have not figured out how to fit it into their spending plan, it is only a matter of time before the plan falls apart.

I want to mention that, in the case just described, of the child not properly managing her income, the parents did not employ any of these steps until the teen was sixteen and working a part-time job. Prior to this point, the teen had been given an allowance, and pretty much whatever spending money she asked for.

When the child got a typical part-time job, the parents began to try to implement a plan similar to what I am building up here. Most teens have no prior experience dealing with these kinds of decisions and hardly want to start. They expect their parents to bail them out and are not only surprised when the demand is placed on them, but become angry when it doesn't happen.

HOARDING ISN'T RIGHT

A cautionary note regarding children managing money: Some kids will tend to hoard their money. You will need to remind them that money is a tool to help us make our way through life, and it's a very good thing to save up; but it is not good to hoard money. Spending is just as important as saving, as it's not a realistic idea to hoard your finances, as most often through life this won't be achievable.

A tool that is not used is of no value. Money is a tool to purse. Money is the instrument that helps us accomplish our purpose or assignment. Money is like a spoon, a tool that you use to eat food so your body is healthy; so you want to get the tool. Spoon is not the main thing, it is a tool. The same with education; it is a tool to help render products and services better, to develop the mind etc.

In the same vein, money is a vehicle or tool. If money is not serving as a tool to help fulfil assignments, then, rather than serve a useful purpose, it becomes harmful, as it eventually enslaves and destroys those who have it.

To minimise the potential for hoarding money, be sure when you set up a spending plan with your child that there are things that have to be purchased by them. As stated in my earlier book, 101 *Tips for Child Development*, give them just enough to force them to have to choose. This will help to reduce the hoarding tendency. One of the indicators that they are hoarding is if they are inclined to shift spending onto others, like you or another sibling or friend.

I have seen families that have one child that spends money on anything and everything in an effort to be liked, or simply because they like to spend money; and a second child with a hoarding bent. The hoarder will gladly let the spendthrift pay for everything while the hoarder stockpiles money. A well designed spending plan helps to control both of these extremes.

AVOIDING DEBT

Debt is something everybody should want to avoid [4]. An extremely important note to therefore consider is: Teach your children that if they don't spend more than they have, they will never be in debt. This can start at surprisingly young ages. Even if you have sat down with your children and have helped them to put together a really good spending plan, there is always the temptation to spend tomorrow's income today. For kids, guess who the bank is. Very likely it is you. Be aware, if you have refused to be the financier of their allowances, they will often hit relatives and friends up for this "cash advance".

Getting into debt is pretty easy, getting out is where the challenge is; it's never easy. My husband and I work with several young people and families to help them get back on track. As your child learns the ropes of managing their income, they will gain confidence and increased self-esteem. You will be equipping them for a greater chance of being successful as adults.

Georgina asked her parents about Christmas presents. She asked why her best friend Tarni received £500 worth of Christmas presents last year but she didn't even receive half of what Tarni got. Georgina was confused because Tarni's mum didn't work, but both Georgina's parents did. Georgina wondered how Tarni's mum could afford it.

Georgina's parents then had to explain the financial situation of Tarni's mum - somebody who was frivolous with her spending and over Christmas would typically spend more than she had, just to make sure her child had plenty of presents.

In explaining the situation thoroughly, Georgina's parents were able to reinforce just how important it is to only spend what you have, rather than getting into debt over trivial things. Georgina then understood how Tarni's mum was careless with her spending, and that's the only reason why she got more than her for Christmas.

2

TEACHING KIDS FINANCIAL MANAGEMENT

If it ever bothered your mind that cramming so much into the brain of a child about finances will be over tasking their psychomotor unnecessarily, then I need to tell you not to underestimate their capacity either. Kids begin to learn from the things they interact with from quite early in life.

I can assure you that children come to know about money from very early in life. With their little fingers they point at the things they like when they stroll the aisles with you at the shopping mall. They see you pick up a product and pay for it at the checkout. In their subconscious they know that money is exchanged for goods we need. So talking about money with kids is not over labouring their brains at all.

You can start at any age, but starting between four and six years old is the ideal age for most kids. At that age, kids are old enough to understand, but not too old to be unyielding.

GOOD OUTLOOK TO LIFE

If your child's worldview is internally centred and focused on their immediate gratification, that child will grow up tending to associate their worth to what they do or don't have. As they have more money and things, they will tend to feel more secure and better about their circumstances. Conversely, they will feel less secure, more anxious, and under greater stress as their income and savings decrease.

Your children's worth is not related to what they have; it's about who they are. As they change their focus from an internal view to the world outside and long range plans and goals, they will begin to feel better about themselves and the world around them. One way to do this is to find a Charity that helps kids of their age group. You may also get someone they can relate to, which makes it real.

There are many good choices, both locally and internationally. It does not have to be a donation of money. In fact, it is best if it is the use of their time and abilities. Most communities have outreach services to the homeless, the less fortunate and infirm. With most children, once they see how well off they have in comparison to others, not only will they want to help out with their time and energy, but will also desire to help out financially.

USING MONEY WELL

Money is a tool to be used. There is nothing magical about it; it doesn't have great powers nor is it more special than any other tool. It has a specific purpose, and when used within the bounds of that purpose, money can be very effective in making our lives less stressful.

Money is a way devised over time to help us keep track of transactions. Sometimes the transaction is our time and effort exchanged for purchasing power (money). Other times it is for tracking the actual purchase of goods or services. Its power, like any other tool, is derived from the person using it. Like a hammer or pair of pliers, money can be used for our benefit or detriment. It all depends on our attitudes, abilities, and intents.

As a parent, a key responsibility of yours is to help your children learn the benefits and drawbacks associated with money. If you can help them to learn that money comes from invested effort and wise decisions, they will begin to appreciate money for what it is, as a tool that is itself "bought" with their energy, time and talents.

Helping children to learn how to maximise their time by choosing wisely when making that exchange can go a long way to improving their confidence, self-esteem and sense of wellbeing. If wise decisions are not made, one becomes overwhelmed and out of control with foreboding anxiety.

MONEY MUST BE EARNED

When your children think that your finances are endless, they will happily spend every single penny you have - and still ask for more when you're done. They will learn to cajole you, pester you, threaten you, publicly embarrass you, and do whatever else they can to get you to part with your hard earned cash to get what they want. Imagine the four-year-old who went shopping with his mum at the mall yelling for something he wants at whatever cost.

You will therefore need to teach your kids that money comes from hard work, perseverance, skill and talent [5] - and that a combination of those qualities will give them their best chance of success. Work is what you create. Work is a pleasure, not punishment. There is pleasure beholding your work of creation. Work is calling purpose to be fulfilled, and it's something that satisfies you. Such delightful work is whatever you get satisfaction from doing.

When you work you make things happen, and derive great pleasure from that, not just the money you earn doing your work; the money does not matter to you as much as the pleasure you derive from what you do. Kids must be encouraged to derive pleasure from work and learn to serve freely. As they do so freely, they discover their skills and develop the skills so that they are in demand. They can then go to university to add value to the discovered skill and bring it to the best level.

THE HELEN'S STORY

Helen had been a caring person from four years old. She had always wanted to be a nurse; she plays nurse and doctor games and consciously watches YouTube videos on her interest to improve herself continually as a nurse. She spends all her time, reading, and helping people; because, for her, it is a passion, for she found her purpose for existence on time. She never did any of her services for money. She always wanted to please God with the gift she has, and care so much for the people, especially the sick, and thinks about how best to care for them.

By this disposition, Helen was able to set herself free from work that makes others to labour just because they need the money. She discovered her passion and found how she could add value to herself. She developed her skills and made herself so valuable that she became highly in demand because she was able to offer quality care service to others.

Helen's passion and calling corresponded with her skills. She worked for the government hospital for a while to develop herself enough; then after five years she started her own practice. She was able to work at her own pace and to obey the dictates of her conscience. She was happy because she started working for her passion. Many people are not so happy because what they are doing is not their passion. Helen's passion was what gave her money; it was her hobby, and she became master of money.

She was able to save some money for three years before taking the next step of investing in her own practice. Thereafter, she stopped working for money, but sends money to work for her, thus becoming master over money. Money ceased to command her to go to work, thereby depriving her of holidays for those three years. Now, she can take her holiday anytime she likes because she has mastered money.

MASTER OVER MONEY

Only those with too much money, or those that don't need money as they have no outgoings, can be the masters of their finances. When you don't have to work because there is need to earn money, only then are you a master over money; only then is money your tool. Or, when you have too much money and that you don't even know what you'd spend it all on. When you use £10 to get petrol for your car or to do other stuff, these are the times when the power you have over your finances can be diminished.

If you truly are a master of your finances, you may wish to spend £100 in an investment to yield for a couple of years of interest, in return to do what your passion is. Without money to pursue your passion, a couple of things could be hard.

There are times when things are not within your control, and may not always work out perfectly. However, if you can begin to help your child grasp the concept of what money is, where it comes from, and how to get it, they will be better prepared for those times when things don't go as planned.

Directly connected to their view of money is how they get it. If you simply dole it out as allowances or in other unearned ways, they would come to expect it from you. Associate their income to assigned responsibilities as part of the family. The starting point for this step is figuring out how much you are already spending on them. Based on their age, abilities, and how far along they are on the path of financial progress. Specifically attach a portion of that amount directly to these assigned responsibilities.

Sit down with them and work through a spending plan for their income. The minimum categories should be Savings, General Expenses, and Charitable Giving. As your child matures in this area, re-evaluate their plan and help them make adjustments.

TIPS FOR CONTROLLING MONEY

The following tips will help you train your child to have mastery over money:

1. Allow Them to Manage Money:

After you and your child have established the source of their income, give them the responsibility of managing it [6]. This can only be done after they have received an education in personal finance. Yes, they will make mistakes, but it's important to let them. It's far better that they do this now, than later in life when those mistakes really count, and can be disastrous.

2. You Must Be Able to Say No:

Saying "No" to bailing your child out of particular financial situations can be one of the more difficult steps for training him or her on financial mastery. It is related to the previous step of letting them manage money by themselves. If you can't say no, they won't learn what you teach them, and will be unable to resist that impulse purchase that can wreak havoc on their spending plan. Keeping finances away from children can make lead them down a path to more frivolous spending when they are old enough to earn their own money and then have the opportunity to spend it.

3. Savings Will Save Them from Disaster:

When money is handed to a child, they must already be knowledgeable of the importance of self-finances, in order to control the instinct, appetite and taste for spending; and this will make kids wealthy inside. Children must:

- Overcome the materialism that comes with money, and the modern day pressures of consumerism.
- Overcome the power of instinct before becoming grown up.

Saving will help them learn to control the pressure to buy what they don't need. It will control the push of money which makes people not to have money.

Especially in society today, where social media is very accessible and more popular than ever before, children are becoming more materialistic. Impulse purchasing is more frequent than ever before in this digital age, and buying things on a whim for 'likes', 'comments' and 'follows' is commonplace. Savings may just save them from any disasters that may have otherwise been caused by this. Just ensure they have a clear understanding of why we keep savings for emergencies and important life events.

JOE'S EXAMPLE

Joe wanted to buy a toy for £5 when he visited the White Rose Shopping Centre, Leeds, with his mum. He had his savings of five pounds but wanted his mum to use her money to buy it. Although he asked his mum nicely, she replied, "A toy does not cost much, just five pounds; but a million pounds is lots of five pounds put together in the same savings pot." He requested to use the money from his wallet instead, but mum advised otherwise, reinforcing her point about saving where you can afford to.

Everything small becomes big, if you keep it up for long enough. Spending £5 per week doesn't sound like much, but that's £260 across the year. That is the point Joe's mum wished to make. Everything adds up. When you continue to save what you have, you will have bigger money in a matter of time. When it is big enough, you can then invest it, and the returns you get from that investment can be used to buy the toy. Hence you retain your initial saving. When you can manage small things, they become big. If you save five pounds a month, that will make thousands of money in 10 years. No amount of money is too small to save or invest. As we saw earlier, even £5 a week can soon add up to a sizeable sum.

Saving a small sum every now and then will not make you rich, but saving consistency, regularly and over a long period of time, will. Most things we buy for our children are not necessary; the money can be saved. Kids must love us not based on gifts, but on life values that we imparted in them while they are in our care.

Saving serves two purposes for most young kids. First, it is used for a planned "big ticket" item such as a nice toy, bicycle or car. The second purpose is for the unplanned events and expenses they encounter. Without both parts, the spending plan is pretty much doomed to failure and frustration.

4. Giving It Away Will Help Them Grow:

Use charitable giving of both their time and income to teach children there is a much bigger world out there, and they have the ability to make a difference. Teach them the invaluable attitude of "I can make a difference." Give them the power to make a difference with money, promote healthy spending, saving and giving.

5. It's OK to Talk about Money:

It's okay to talk about money [7]. Include your children in some of the family's money decisions. Keep it simple, and base it on their ability to understand it. It's not necessary to show them your pay stubs. Give them the bank statements or the family spending plan. Just give them a chance to have input on some basic spending decisions.

6. Tell Them about Your Choices:

Tell your children about some money mistakes you made. Maybe it was a "Get-Rich-Quick" plan that didn't work out so well. Tell them about some of the things you got right, like refinancing the mortgage so you can get it paid off earlier and save several thousands of pounds or dollars. They will appreciate the trust you have shown them.

SEE JUDE AND JACK

Jude told his son Jack about Forex trading which his friend introduced him to, and how he found out by his experience that it was not a good business for him. He said he will not advise his son to go into it as he now sees it as gambling, and the easiest way to lose money. "Don't be in a hurry to make money; you will lose money that way," he told Jack.

People who want to defraud you know you want to make money quick. For example, MLM and forex are not for money making, nor is network marketing a good way to make money either, as only those at the top of the pecking order make the money. Save consistently and discipline your desires. It is not how much you save but how much you spend.

7. Teach Them about Compounded Interest:

The "magic" of compounded interest can help your children achieve their goals much sooner, just as the reverse can bury their goals in financial bondage. At their young age, this is generally not an issue, but if they can learn it now, it could make a big difference in their future.

8. Don't Give Up, and Don't Give In:

No matter what tactics your children might use to wear you down, it is important for you to stand strong. Kids can really take their toll on your mental and physical wellbeing if you let them, but if you don't give in, eventually they will understand they are wasting their time and energy, and find that life is much better using a different approach.

JOHN AND JACK

John, 49, from Wakefield, was falling victim to the wide-eyed requests of his grandson, Jack. Jack, who John wished to please (as it was his first grandchild and sought his affection at every given moment), would always give in after the third or fourth plea for a new toy in the shop.

"Please granddad John, I really like Ben 10" he would say, over and over again. Wide-eyed, knowing his Granddad would eventually cave, Jack knew exactly how to play the situation.

John unfortunately couldn't stand strong, until his daughter (Jack's mother) imparted her wisdom on him. She informed him that the only reason he does it is because he knows his granddad will cave and buy him the toy. So, John's daughter told him to stand strong and don't give in, saying "He will soon realise he's wasting his time and energy and he'll give up."

3

LEARN TO SAY NO

Let's start with an example. Your child is saving to pay the fee to play a sports game, and then decides to spend the savings on the latest games console game. It's OK for you to remind the child that they are saving up so they can play sports. Then help them to come to the conclusion that by making the choice to buy the game, they will not have enough to play the sport. It is better if they can think through this on their own with some coaching from you. If you tell them they can't immediately have the video game, it will not have the same impact; and they are less likely to own the decision.

It's okay to say no every now and then [8]. You are not the bad guy for doing so.

If they choose to spend the money on that game, you need to let them. Of course this will depend on the age and ability of the child. For younger children, I would not make a sport's fee a part of their income.

When it comes time for the sport's fee and they don't have the funds to cover it, you will need to let them not play the sport for that season.

Yes, as a parent, it will be tough to allow your child to bear the result of their decisions, and may even be an additional burden on you. But they will learn several very powerful lessons. They will discover that money is limited in its supply; that all choices we make have trade-offs; and they are responsible to manage the decisions they make.

If you choose to bail them out, you will be teaching them equally powerful lessons. You will be teaching them that you really don't mean what you say. They will begin to view your words more as a suggestion than meaning what you say. You will be teaching them that they don't have to be responsible for their choices. You will be teaching them that as long as someone else has money, they will get bailed out. And you will be demonstrating to them that our choices don't really matter because someone else will cover for us.

Having a good, solid spending plan will give your children a guide for making spending decisions. It will help them to make informed decisions and to prioritise what's important to them. It will teach them that impulse purchases have effects beyond the moment.

Your kids need to learn to say "No" as well. When faced with that impulse purchase or opportunity, they need to ask the question, "Is it in my spending plan?" If it is not, then don't buy it. If they still want it, you need to let them make that decision. But, with that decision they should be able to demonstrate to you how they are going to work it into the spending plan. If they can't, it is still their decision and you need to let them learn the hard lesson of not participating in that sport they traded it for.

If they really do want it, I believe having them figure out how they will work it into their spending plan is the better approach. First, have them wait for three days before making the decision to buy. If they still want it, have them make the appropriate changes to their spending plan and begin to set aside a portion of their income into the savings category until they save up enough to buy the game for their console.

MORE WORK FOR MONEY

Another option is for them to try to figure out how to come up with the additional needed money. This may mean taking on additional jobs around the house, or maybe in the neighbourhood. Here in the UK, this isn't quite as common, but is certainly worth a try if you have elderly neighbours who may need a hand every now and then. If your child chooses to do jobs around the house, don't make it too easy on them to achieve their goal.

Your child will learn that if it is worth having, it is worth the wait and work invested. The time invested will make the reward so much sweeter. They will learn the value of saving for the future. In many instances, they will decide after a time that the Xbox game wasn't such a great idea after all, and end up not buying it. The lesson here is that impulse purchases can be far more costly than the purchase price. In this example, the opportunity of playing sports was nearly lost to a fleeting whim to have that game.

Remember, a spending plan is basically a priority list. If your child deciding to have that new game is more important than playing sports, then so be it.

Of course there will be times when you have to step in and stop the transaction. But these should be the rare exceptions.

One of the most important things we can get them to learn is to ask the question, "Is this purchase something I have allowed for in my spending plan?" If the answer is "No", then don't buy it. If you can teach your children this concept, they will be well on their way to a less stressful adult life.

It may seem to you that I have not given adequate attention to this step. It is just that simple. If you and your child have followed the guidance so far, then you have answered the How-much-is-enough question, and built a spending plan. By doing this, you have said this is how much we have to work with, and these are the priorities.

Plans and priorities change, but any of these changes should be based on well thoughtout goals and not on an impulsive reaction. Learning to say "No" to these impulses will keep you and your child on the path of progress.

LUCY AND LAYNE

Lucy, 32, from Newcastle, reinforced the points above with her daughter Layne from a very young age. She taught the importance of understanding the word 'no' and why you shouldn't reroute your life over potentially-pointless purchases.

"Learning self-control is important" Lucy explained.

"That's why I have a spending plan, here, take a look" she continued.

Lucy proceeded to show Layne her detailed spending plan that she kept on her smartphone, and the importance of staying on-route with your finances, instead of allowing impulse purchases to take control. Layne learnt all about spending plans from a very young age and will therefore be wiser with her spending habits as she becomes old enough to manage her own finances.

4

MONEY AND KIDS

Money isn't scarce, at least in the mind of a child. Children have endless amounts of purchasing power (in billions, even if in their minds only), resources they believe are available to them directly or indirectly. Yet, they are rarely taught about money, or more importantly, the management of money. Some parents are as guilty as the next parent on making it a point to teach their kids about money and money management skills.

THE MYSTERY OF MONEY

Of course, the generation gap combined with the technology age in which kids now live has a big part in lack of focus on this subject. But no more. If for no other reason, you should think for a moment how money is so rapidly transferred today, with just the swipe of a card. And in fact, many people (parents) today hardly ever come in contact with actual paper money anymore.

It's so easy to load up your shopping basket with just the swipe of a card; but there lies the trouble for kids and managing their money today. It's just too easy and there's no immediate pain of actually taking those hard earned pounds/dollars out of your little purse or wallet and parting with your money at the time of the purchase.

First, don't put off teaching your kids about money, the value of it, and how to manage it. It's never too early, in our day and time. When you first begin to acquaint your child with money, be prepared for mistakes and some growing pains understanding the concept of money. It is far better to allow your children to learn from mistakes involving small amounts rather than later in life when the same mistakes can prove financially disastrous. Many financial experts agree that a big mistake is for parents not to allow their children to have control over their money early on.

TEACHING MONEY VALUE

As with teaching children about any subject matter, there are general guidelines about the level of complexity that is introduced at any particular age; teaching your kids about money management is certainly no exception [9]. So, let's take a look at some general teaching guidelines pertaining to money management and at what age level.

Even with toddlers and preschoolers you can give your child an allowance. Now keep in mind that they will probably play with it, misplace it, and maybe even lose it; but that's perfectly fine. At this age, it is merely introducing the concept that their little bit of money has value and should be kept safe so it will be around when they want to use it.

With the ease and power given to today's consumer, it is difficult to get adults to understand and have the discipline to save for something they want or need to purchase. But even at an age as early as about first year/grade you should begin to take on this challenge with your child — so much of today is instant gratification. And no philosophy will be tougher for you to overcome with your children and money management as this. Delayed gratification or saving for something they want is a very difficult concept to teach kids, and for kids to master; but it is one of the most important things to do to enable them manage their money.

Be sure to continue on with working with your children the delayed gratification concept. In other words, teach them the principle of working and saving for something that they want to get. You'll find (and they will too) that as they learn this lesson, whatever it is they worked, waited and saved for will have much greater value to them personally.

Be sure to check out various online tools and games that can help with teaching the value of money.

BETWEEN NEED AND WANT

The next level you'll want to discuss with and teach your kids are the difference between 'need' and 'want'. This is ever so important today in this media, marketing and consumption society in which we live and our kids are hammered with daily. You won't have to look far for examples of needs versus wants. Just turn on the TV and wait for an advertisement, and now it doesn't even need to be this way. Your child can pick up a tablet or smartphone and each and every application, social media platform and website will display some form of advertising – some of which they are bound to be interested in.

Talk with your kids and discuss what it is the advertisement is going after them for, and why. This is a considerable money management accomplishment for kids when they begin to honestly differentiate between needs and wants.

It's also at this point (early to mid-grade school) that your kids begin to establish some sort of savings plan for something they would like to have (notice I didn't use 'want'). The whole process of budgeting and saving for something at this age will give your kids a great sense of accomplishment, pride, and a first start toward financial confidence. Also at this age, with your kids introduced to saving and budgeting, it is a good time to introduce them to paying for some of the extras that they would like to have for school, sports, band, etc, and for beginning charitable contribution.

From here continue increasing your kid's understanding of budgeting and managing their money by weaning them off from you providing the lion's share of their 'wants', to them working, budgeting, and saving. Simply increase their financial responsibility to them; keep increasing their social responsibility too by giving to charities of yours and their choice.

GROWING INTO FINANCIAL FREEDOM

As your kids progress to their teen years and become more mature, the time will come that you may want to consider getting your child some form of debit card. By this time in their life they'll be considering university or some career path that will quite possibly require some sort of financial allowances/student loan, and at the very least they will be needing even more financial freedom.

A prepaid parent-monitored debit card is an initial good solution. By now, and through these many years of your tutelage, your child has become financially literate and it's all because you started early on teaching your child solid money management skills and attitude.

Do you know you can bring to your kid's knowledge that they too can start earning money for themselves? Never make them believe that without you around them they can't achieve anything. While they grow, each of them has unique trait that makes one different from the other. So, the moment you identify that, let them use that to keep themselves busy, while at the same time making money out of such a service.

A MOTIVATED PHOTOGRAPHER

Emily walked up to her mum one sunny afternoon, requesting that she gets enrolled for a photography class. She was attentive in class, and in no time graduated in flying colours. That skill would have deteriorated were it not for her father's intervention, having invited her for a photo session at his place of work. The end of the year's party was so thrilling that after the party, Emily was appreciated and given stipends. She was highly commended for her creativity during the event. Since then, she had taken that serious to the extent that in her school, she, most times, feature as the school's photographer.

Beyond making resources from what started so little in her father's office, Emily took some shots about nature which people appreciated and paid for. All these she did during her holidays.

As parents, invest in your children's creativity and allow them to make out resources from that. With that, they won't just be financially free; they'll also enjoy what they do passionately. Your children's interests may be found in making of hair, tutoring, coffee shops or carwash, social media influencer, Paper boy or newspaper rounds, helping at the corner shops to distribute newspapers to the old people in the morning before they go to school, which will fetch them a couple of coins/notes at the end of the week. This will go a far-reaching way in decreasing the rate at which they will see you as their lifeline. Also, they'll see themselves as being responsible more than others.

All they will ever need in life is whatever it is that will make them feel free to express themselves. Hence, if they are accountable for the choices they make, they'd see more reasons to do what they needed to do well at the appropriate time.

A LIST OF POSSIBILITIES

There are countless possibilities of money earning activities kids at different ages can engage their creativities in this modern age. My list here is not exhaustive.

1. Event planning for their own programmes

2. Headgear tie for events
3. YouTube uploads
4. Blogging
5. Social media influencer
6. Logo design
7. Game design and development
8. Graphic design
9. Poster and Flyer design and distribution
10. Banner ad
11. Photoshop editing
12. T-shirt design and presentation
13. Modelling
14. Music
15. Web traffic
16. Translating and interpreting other languages
17. Animation for kids
18. Comics Producer and composer
19. Video editing
20. Viral video
21. Making of greeting cards
22. Data entry
23. Mobile app

Depending on their age and exposure, kids get to take pleasure in some of these activities anyway, and earning money doing any of these is added fun.

GREGG

Gregg was a talented artist and had a love for fashion. At the young age of 14, he had already designed his own t-shirt. Though, he was doing this solely for his own personal benefit, giving him something unique.

His father, however, insisted that he learn the value of money and put his entrepreneurial skills to work, challenging him to turn his talent into a viable business. He promised that there would be a 'reward' for his efforts by the end.

Little did Gregg know; the reward would be the money he would make from his school friends after the t-shirt business was successful. His father pushed him to utilise his 'possibility' and make his own money, and that's exactly what Gregg did.

Not only did this teach Gregg valuable skills in terms of personal finance, but it strengthened his entrepreneurial skills, toughened him to the real-world of earning money and prepared him for later life.

5

SAVINGS

Everyone has the opportunity to do something with their money; some squander money and soon fall under its control, while those who master money save and invest it till when it can serve a better use.

THE COMING RAINY DAY

Savings will save your child from a future financial disaster. For kids, there are generally two reasons for saving money. One reason is to save up for a specific purchase, like a toy, a bicycle, a game system, a car or university. The second reason is to be prepared for unexpected purchases [10]. Mastering how to save will help to convert a spending plan disaster to a simple decision.

The first reason: saving for a particular "big ticket" item, should be built into the spending plan. The money is set aside for a specific purpose — this is teaching your child long range planning. Using the comparison shopping skills you have taught them, they would decide how much they will need to make this purchase. Then using the spending plan, they are able to figure out how much they need to save out of each income source to get to that goal in a given time frame.

A cautionary note: As mentioned in the chapter on learning to say no, impulse buying can delay or even derail this part of the plan. When your child sees something they want right now, and then remembers they have this money saved up, they will be tempted to act on impulse and spend the savings for a purchase that the money was not intended for. This is where you will need to remind them of their goal and the purpose of the money.

An essential tactic to reduce this impulse, is to have that money stashed away in a bank account or a place that is not easily accessed. Many people choose to invest their money in ISA accounts and premium bonds. These cannot easily be accessed but are there when/if you really need them – allowing you to keep a decent sum behind you, whilst earning interest. In terms of premium bonds, you also have the chance to win monthly sums of money too.

Your children should not have the money on them. Unless they are ready to make the purchase for which the money was intended, it needs to be tucked away safely.

Do not be their "Ready Cash" or "Pay Day Loan" machine. What I mean by this is, you will most likely be asked, or you may even feel like you want to "help" them out and "loan" them the money until you get home. Avoid this impulse. You want them to learn how to resist this type of buying and to learn how to make the wiser purchases.

The second reason for saving money is to be prepared for those unforeseen expenses. For example, it may be that unplanned trip to the water park with a friend or the above mentioned impulse purchase. For an older child it might be they lost their mobile/cell phone and want to replace it. Again, you would not want your child to have this money on them. If it is in their pockets, they are far more likely to spend it on something other than intended. It should be tucked away safely. This enforces a waiting period, which helps to reduce poor purchasing decisions.

WHY HOARDING HURTS

Another caution: Some kids tend to hoard their money unnecessarily. Though this sounds like it could only be a positive thing, in fact, it can unfortunately be as bad as not having any kind of spending plan at all. Hoarding has a tendency to lead to an attitude of arrogance. As they pile up more and more money, they will start to feel they are better than others.

Another danger in hoarding is the anxiety it can cause. As your child builds up this cash pile, they begin to attach their worth to it, and feel happier about it as it grows; and when it comes time to spend it, as the pile of money goes down, they could become more and more anxious. The amount of money stocked up becomes the barometer for their mood. As the amount increases, so does their sense of security; as it decreases, they become anxious, moody, feeling insecure.

To keep your kids feeling like they don't have as

much, they will resist spending it, and even try to find ways to transfer their expenses to others. Having a good, solid spending plan helps to alleviate this improper response to money.

MORE THAN MONEY

Good as money is, it must not be your primary source of joy and happiness. If anything is giving you joy other than true love of God, then that thing will spoil in your hand. Having Love should be your primary source of joy and happiness, not money. Kids must be free from making physical things to determine their source of joy and happiness. Our real wealth is knowing true love of God, but people gravitate towards physical things that are visible to identify.

Some kids work for money because they want to have a better identity, looking at how much money they are worth and how much physical things they have. This is why they want to increase the physical things they have. This attitude encourages pride.

Kim always daydreams about how much money would be given to her by her rich uncle. But when the uncle finally arrives and gives her a fiver, she gets so disappointed because she had daydreamed on getting £100, just because the uncle is rich. She had looked forward to pleasure herself on what she wanted to buy.

Kim was disappointed and felt unhappy because she let her joy to depend on the money she expected from someone. She ought to know that rich people tend to be very frugal with their money because they worked hard for it. She ought to have asked her uncle to give her an opportunity to use her skills and work in his establishment both to improve her skills and earn something for self. It is the sort of request rich people like to respond to.

It is the sort of thing that adds value to oneself and makes one rich inside, thereby increasing one's worth. It makes one to be valued by others, and it always pays better than largesse doled out by benevolent people.

BOB

Bob had a somewhat unpleasant experience in his life, in which he bumped into somebody he went to school with, some twenty years ago. Fred, his childhood friend, was only speaking about the things he had bought, like his brand-new Range Rover, his six-bedroom house and his newly-designed cinema room.

As good as money can be for somebody, Bob knew that Fred's primary source of happiness was his substantial bank balance and the things he could therefore afford to buy. In seeing how Fred talked about money, Bob acknowledged and knew all the reasons why he should never fall into that trap.

Bob's happiness came from his family, and that was only reinforced due to his interaction with Fred – who was very materialistic and was relying on money and belongings to fill certain emotional voids in his life.

BUILDING A SPENDING PLAN

What if I titled this Chapter, "Money Costs Money"? It would explain my intention here, wouldn't it? Because your child's financial training is like going on a long trip without a map. You might get there eventually, but the number of unintended detours, backtracking and wrong turns along the way will cost you in time and money.

There's also the frustration and insecurity of not knowing if you are in a safe place or even if you are travelling in the right direction. It is only a well-designed spending plan, like a good map, that will make the journey go a lot smoother.

SPENDING MAP FOR CHILDREN

Having a spending plan teaches your child the value of saving for "big ticket" items – that special toy they really want, a gift for a family member, fees for their sports clubs and social activities with their friends, for example – while at the same time managing the day-to-day expenses – a chocolate bar at the checkout line, a drink and a burger at the local football game, or App Store download. It reinforces and helps them to learn priority-setting.

There are few things in life that reflect a person's priorities more than how they spend their money. To paraphrase what I once heard someone say, "Let me see how you spend your money and take a look at what you throw away, and I can tell a lot about what is important to you." A spending plan forces us to realise what's important to us.

For younger children, you should help them to set up a very basic spending plan. Have one fund to save for those big ticket items like the bicycle they really want. Have another fund for general spending, the day-to-day items like the chocolate bar at the supermarket checkout or a small toy. Have them set up a third fund for charitable giving. If you have a special Charity you support, let them pitch in.

For example, here is Compassion UK link. https://www.compassionuk.org/sponsorship/

Involving children makes it more real for them. It is important that our children understand that life exists beyond ourselves, and that sometimes we can be a part of helping someone else in their time of need.

If you are starting this with a younger child, the one thing that works well is to get a three part bank that is labeled for spending, savings, and charity. When pay day comes around, teach them to put at least 10% in the savings bank, 10% in the charity bank, and the remainder in the spending bank. If you are going to have them make the purchases for birthday gifts for friends or family members, have them put more than 10% in the savings portion. Having them buy the gifts is a good idea because it gives them a feeling of happiness and fulfilment if they are directly involved in the giving.

Regardless of where the money comes from, whether it is income from you or a gift from a grandparent, teach them to divide it into the three categories. This will keep them from seeing money as anything other than the tool that it is. If it is given to them for a specific purchase – say, grandma gave them the money as a birthday gift toward the purchase of a new bike – then all of it would be placed in the bank associated with that purchase. In this example, it would all go into the savings bank.

SPENDING MAP FOR TEENS

As your child approaches secondary/high school the categories will be more complex. Many people have talked about having a "Miscellaneous" category. I recommend you avoid it. What we have seen happen over the years is that a lot of things get dumped here when they should belong somewhere more specific. If you feel you must have this category, teach your teen to use it sparingly and watch it closely.

With older children you can do a realistic evaluation of the cost of everything you and your child can think of to meet their basic needs and longterm goals. Include everything you would probably be paying for anyway. Depending on their previous involvement, it is quite likely that your two lists won't match exactly. Don't worry about it, start with everything you both can think of, then work backwards.

Once you have compiled the list, review it in relation to your child's age and ability to grasp the concepts. Decide what they are ready to take on and what you should keep. Don't be afraid to stretch a little; this is how they grow. Because we want to maintain control, most parents do not give their children sufficient responsibility. Resist this urge.

Remember, this should be a "zero-sum" event for you. You should not be giving them any more than what you would have spent on them in the first place. The only real difference is how it gets managed, and by whom. Be prepared for a surprise. You will likely discover that you are buying a lot more than you think.

THE NEED FOR SUPERVISION

In the beginning, keep a close eye on how your child is doing. This is a critical point in the process; it establishes the foundation for their future success. As your child demonstrates an ability to manage and make right decisions you can give over more control. If you began at an early age, by the time they are ready for secondary/high school you will have a pretty good idea of how they will do.

As your child matures it will be necessary to make adjustments: to alter the amount given, the categories, and responsibilities along the way. It is all part of your child learning how responsibility is related to privilege. Strictly from a parenting position, it is easier to increase the money than decrease it, and it is easier to reduce the responsibilities than increase them. Do not let ease and personal comfort overshadow the growing opportunity this experience provides your child.

Of all of the steps, this one is the most important. If your child enters adulthood understanding how to manage what they have, it won't matter as much about their income. Why? They will know how to be successful with whatever they have. Teach your kids how to build their own map to a more victorious money management plan. When they become adults, they will be far better prepared to meet the challenges that defeat many families everyday.

ZOE

Zoe's mum documented her daughter's financial education journey. Noting any changes that she made to her ability to comprehend the importance of finance, any decisions she was able to make and how her attitude towards money changed. This can be found underneath and comprises of several snippets from the journal.

Age 5 – Taught Zoe that money is not endless.

Age 6 – Began to give Zoe pocket money. Reinforced the importance of saving, and how she can get something 'big' with her money if she doesn't spend it for a long period of time.

Age 9 – Zoe is becoming more materialistic. I continue to reinforce the importance of saving. Little success. Hopefully she learns from her mistakes.

Age 13 – Zoe now has social media. Sponsored posts are giving her wild ideas about what to spend her money on.

7

WAYS TO TEACH KIDS ABOUT MONEY

Teaching Kids could be great fun; that's if you know how. Those who don't easily get frustrated and abandon the business altogether. Let me offer some simple technics for teaching children, especially the very tender ones.

TEACHING PRE-SCHOOLERS AND KINDERGARTNERS ABOUT MONEY

This is the most fun group of kids to teach. Here is how:

1. USE A CLEAR JAR TO SAVE.

The piggybank is a great idea, but it doesn't give kids

a visual. When you use a clear jar, they see the money growing. Yesterday, they had a pound/dollar bill and five dimes. Today, they have a pound/dollar bill, five dimes and a quarter! Talk through this with them and make a big deal about it growing!

Every thing small becomes big. When you continue to save what you have you will have bigger money in a matter of time. When it is big enough, you can then invest it, and the returns you get from that investment can be spent; hence you retain your initial saving. When you can manage small things, they become big. If you pay the price of waiting for it to grow, you will get the best. Interestingly, kids this age can understand what the clear jar demonstrates.

2. SET AN EXAMPLE

A study found that money habits in children are formed by the time they're seven years old. They can see your example and will do as you do. So bear in mind always, little eyes are watching you. If you're slapping down plastic every time you go out to dinner or the grocery store, they'll eventually notice. Or if you and your spouse are arguing about money, they'll notice that too. Set a healthy example for them and they'll be much more likely to follow it when they get older.

3. SHOW THEM THAT STUFF COSTS MONEY

You've got to do more than say, "That pack of toy cars costs £5/ $5, son." Help them grab a few pounds/dollars out of their jar, take it with them to the store, and physically hand the money to the cashier. This simple action will have more impact than a five-minute lecture.

TEACHING ELEMENTARY/PRIMARY PUPILS AND SECONDARY/MIDDLE SCHOOLERS ABOUT MONEY

4. SHOW OPPORTUNITY COST

Opportunity cost is just another way of saying, "If you buy this video game, then you won't have the money to buy that pair of shoes." At this age, your kids should be able to weigh decisions and understand the possible outcomes.

5. GIVE COMMISSIONS, NOT ALLOWANCES

Don't give your kids money for breathing. Pay them commissions based on creative chores they do around the house, like taking out the trash, cleaning their room, or mowing the grass.

Dave and his daughter, Rachel Cruze, talked a lot about this system in their book, *Smart Money Smart Kids.* This concept helps your kids understand that money is earned – it's not just given to them.

6. AVOID IMPULSE BUYS

"Mom, I found this cute dress. It's perfect and I love it! Can we buy it, please?"

Does this sound familiar? This age group really knows how to capitalise on the impulse buy – especially when it uses someone else's money.

Instead of giving in, let your child know they can use their hard-earned commission to pay for it. But encourage your child to wait at least a day before they purchase anything over £10 or $10. It will likely still be there tomorrow, and they'll be able to make that money decision with a level head the next day [11].

7. STRESS THE IMPORTANCE OF GIVING

Once they start making a little money, be sure you teach them about giving. They can pick a church, charity or even someone they know who needs a little help. Eventually, they'll see how giving doesn't just affect the people they give to, but the giver as well.

TEACHING TEENAGERS ABOUT MONEY

8. TEACH THEM CONTENTMENT

Your teen probably spends a good chunk of their time staring at a screen as they scroll through social media. And every second they're online, they're seeing the highlight reel of their friends, family and even total strangers! It's the quickest way to bring on the comparison trap.

Contentment starts in the heart. Let your teen know that their Honda (although not the newest car on the block) is still running well enough to get them from point A to point B. And you can still throw a memorable, milestone birthday dinner/celebration without spending a chunk of your savings funding it!

9. GIVE THEM THE RESPONSIBILITY OF A BANK ACCOUNT

By the time your kid is a teenager, you should be able to set them up with a simple bank account if you've been doing some of the above along the way. This takes money management to the next level, and will, hopefully, prepare them for managing a much heftier account when they get older.

10. GET THEM SAVING FOR UNIVERSITY

There's no time like the present to have your teen start saving for university. Do they plan on working a summer job? Perfect! Take a portion of that (or more) and toss it in a university savings account. Your teen will feel like they have skin in the game as they contribute toward their education.

Putting money in the bank does not particularly make it grow or increase reasonably, but it retains it till it grows to an amount that can be invested. Money in the bank is not for growth, but to make it work for you; and to do that, it must be invested.

Good education is an investment.

LUCAS

Lucas, a 17-year-old boy from southeast London with a passion for graphic design worked at KFC for three consecutive summers because it was close to his house and he was able to save £3,000. The following September, as he went to university, he wanted to grow his graphic design business, so he used £100 to pay for advertising in *Student Union* as a cover artist designer.

In about a week, he received four clients that wanted him to design their song covers. He made £200; and he kept repeating the process and marketing himself on social media. As his clientele grew, his social media following grew. This meant he could decrease his marketing budget because he can market to his clients directly.

With his increased clientele came more earnings, more savings, more investment with greater returns. That's how people become rich. I call it focus thinking, passionate working habit, perseverance and determination to succeed. No one with these qualities go poor.

After a while of working hard, Lucas was able to multiply his initial savings. All of that happening while his friends were still struggling with money because they consumed the amount they had and didn't think of growth and multiplication. On his part, Lucas found a way to make his capital to work for him.

Everyone came to this world with a gift, talent or ability. In his case, Lucas knew he liked to chat with people and wanted to work in an area where his interest could be developed. He did not know his gift or calling specifically yet, though he knew he was somewhat intelligent and had a passion for graphic design. So, he put what he had to good use.

Some kids think they don't have anything, no gifts, no passion, or no money, just because they don't have physical cash. And this is because they have not converted or increased or multiplied their gifts. Kids must use what they have; and by using what they already have, it will increase and bring returns. That's what Lucas did.

Whatever gifts kids have been given is what you are capable to increase or multiply. But you need to prove you are faithful first in the little you already have before you get an increase. If you are not faithful with little then the little you have will be taken away. This is a divine concept (Matthew 25:14-29). The little one has but fails to use is taken away, lest one abuses it, messes it up, throws it away, missuses it, or uses it to endanger oneself. That is why it is safe to take away from you and give to the guy who has proved to be faithful and responsible enough to multiply the little into something worthwhile.

In this scenario, Lucas learnt how to appropriately manage his finances. He used his initial capital to invest in his future, something many will consider to be forward-thinking, with a 'big picture' mindset.

Lucas was unlike his friends, who prefered to keep working than plan for themselves. Lucas would often consider them to be idle, not utilising their talents to the best of their ability, not seizing every opportunity given to them.

See, the common belief is that lazy children work with their hands, but forward-thinking, intelligent children work with their brains. Those who use their brain manage others in the workplace; they hire people who work with their hands and legs. Or, that's how the saying goes, anyway.

More is entrusted to those who have been tested and tried in responsibility, stewardship, frugality and management of money. God expects us to be faithful with money and shrewdness, which is to make the right financial decisions. To be shrewed is to make well informed decisions to get a better result.

Frugality is the ability to be economical with money

so that you can save it, multiply it, and cause it to grow. Frugality is how you demonstrate that you have authority over money. You control it so that you don't come under its slavery; it's how you demonstrate that you are master over money, and not the other way around.

HARRY

Harry was just ten years old when he bought his first Go-Pro camera. This cost a lot of money, but it wasn't simply a frivolous purchase, it was an investment.

See, Harry had been saving his pocket money for some years now. Growing up watching gamers/vloggers on YouTube playing Minecraft and Fortnite, he had long since wanted to become a gamer himself. Luckily, Harry was able to see the 'bigger picture' and noticed that if he saved his £5 pocket money each week for at least a year, he would be able to afford a good Go-Pro to start his own channel – and that's exactly what he did.

Harry quickly became popular and his investment in the Go-Pro camera proved to be worthwhile – as it didn't take long for Harry to reach a wide enough audience that he could monetize his videos. In doing so, he was able to make a steady, regular income from a very young age. His forward-thinking, positive and motivated attitude made him over £500 in his first year as a Minecraft/Fortnite YouTuber.

11. TEACH THEM TO STEER CLEAR OF STUDENT LOANS WHERE POSSIBLE

Some people may not have yet realised, but student loans, though can be very helpful, also have their downfalls. Therefore, where it can be achieved (depending on individual circumstances), they should be avoided.

Before your teen even applies to university, you should likely consider it down and have the talk – the "How are we going to pay for university" talk.

Although universities in the UK provide a lot of help and advice via Student Finance England, it's important to first have a 'plan' of sorts on how you want to approach it but do consider the information on the website.

Let your teen know the later-life implications of student loan, and if it can be avoided, such that if student loans aren't an option to fund their education, it will be a great thing.

Talk through all the alternatives out there, like going to community university, apprenticeship, going to an in-state university, working part-time while in school, and applying for scholarships/bursaries and grants as they apply to different countries and universities.

While you're at it, get Tips for #unilife for them. It's a must-have resource to help our university-bound teen prepare for the next big step in their life.

12. TEACH THEM THE DANGER OF CREDIT CARDS

As soon as your kid turns 18, they'll get hounded by credit card offers – especially once they're in university. If you haven't taught them why debt is a bad idea, they'll become yet another credit card victim. Remember, it's up to you to determine the right time you'll teach them these principles. Just remember this, credit cards can be dangerous [12].

13. GET THEM ON A SIMPLE BUDGET

They should learn the importance of making a plan for their money while they're still under your roof.

14. INTRODUCE THEM TO INVESTMENT OPPORTUNITIES

I know what you're thinking. You can barely get your teens to brush their hair – how in the world are they supposed to become investment savvy?

The earlier your child can get started investing, the better. Investment in their skills will be a good start! Introduce your teen to it at an early age, and they'll get a headstart on preparing for their future.

15. HELP THEM FIGURE OUT HOW TO USE THEIR TIME

When you think about it, teenagers have plenty of free time – whether it's half-terms, Easter, Summer or Christmas. If your teen wants some money (and which teen doesn't?), then help them find a job. Better still, help them become an entrepreneur! These days, it's easier than ever for your teen to start up their own business and turn in profit.

Providing a product or service is essentially what business is in its simplest form. How can kids serve people with their time, talent, and expertise? Have them consider ways they can serve the community.

If necessary, they can begin serving people for free to get them to recognise and discover their value to the community. When they add value, they will always immediately become valuable. Once they have proven themselves, looking for problems to solve and improving on their skills, they can set and negotiate a pay. Make sure to balance the time spent on business with their academic, spiritual, social and other aspects of their life.

YOUNG KIDS AND MONEY

Unfortunately, handling money is not something we learn at school. Just like many other life skills that we find necessary in adulthood, money management is also neglected while lots of energy is spent on secondary/high levels of math.

If you examine the curriculum your kids are covering from prep to Year 13, you can understand why many of them will go to university or get tertiary education, but only one kid per class will be upscale. (Though somes schools in the UK have now started to offer Financial literacy alongside maths) Are you ready to make sure it is your kid?

Handling money is something we all need an awareness and knowledge of, long before we leave the family home. When friends have brand-name shoes or a computer game and your kid wants them too, your kid's ability to understand money is going to be very handy. So, if you wonder when it is the right time to learn about money. My answer is: the minute your kid can count to 10.

LEARNING FROM ANTS

Sam's countenance spoke worry when he approached his Maths teacher, after the bi-weekly lesson. He wondered as he drew closer to Steve. *How could an ant prepare their food in the summer? How could we humans that can easily trample ants under the sole of one's feet now go and learn from an ant?* All these ran through his mind. He was oblivious of the fact that Steve observed he was not the usual Sam – lively and energetic after every lesson – he used to know.

"Sam!" The teacher called out to him.

"Yes, sir!" Sam replied timidly as he continually rubbed his eyes with the back of his hand while he walked wobbly towards the direction of the teacher.

"You look worried. Hope all is well with you?"

"Not at all. I've been thinking about your lesson this

morning, and I seem a little bit confused!" Sam let out the words gently as he looked into the eyes of the teacher. That provoked laughter out of the teacher's mouth.

"Let's take a walk around this place a bit. Do you have some minutes to spare?"

"And my parents?"

"I'll walk you home for them to be rest assured that you've been with me," he assured Sam as they walked at arm's length.

As both of them walked to the school's playground in silence, Sam became more worried. He was anticipating quick responses to the questions of his mind, but none came. After about an hour of intermission of silence, save for the rustling of the leaves they marched through the playground.

Dazed by what the teacher did, he didn't hesitate so long before he did what the teacher did, waiting for what the teacher would do next. The teacher crouched by an old mobile-classroom outdoors. Sam crouched too.

"Do you see this?" he pointed at a lined-up colony of ants, forming rows of ants in their numbers on two sides, while some other multitude walked gallantly in the middle moving crumbs of bread.

Surprised by what he saw, he asked, "Why did some form a wall and are not moving, while those in the middle keep moving?"

"They are protectors of the workers who are in the middle," the teacher said with a shy smile.

"Can't they work? Does that mean they're indolent?" Sam seemed bothered by the teacher's explanation, which wasn't so detailed.

Teacher Steve unleashed raucous laughter from his mouth, "Son, that's what's called responsibility. They're so organised that each one of them in its colony understands its duty and won't leave there, even when faced with challenges."

It really touched Sam's heart that he scattered the line to confirm what the teacher just said. After about half an hour later, he couldn't curtail his delight as he jumped up in amazement to have seen that the ants never bothered about those that lost their lives, as they continued pushing the crumbs forward. He looked up at the teacher and asked, "So, what does this tell us as human, teacher?"

"We need to learn how to save during the day, so that at night, we can sit back and relax to enjoy," teacher Steve said.

"But we usually sleep at night. Or is there any other night you're talking about?" Sam asked innocently.

"The 'night' here means when we're old. Haven't you seen how miserable some people live their lives in their old age?"

"Yes, I have."

"That shows you that while they were still in their teens, they never felt they should save all the money received as incentives from families or parents. Inside the tiny brain of the ants, it thinks it should save for winter by storing up something for the future. And if I may ask you, Sam, how much have you saved so far in this first quarter of the year?" The teacher inquired looking to expunge the truth from Sam.

"I've got few quid before now that I intend saving but spent it for my guitar lesson."

"Another lesson, spend after you save and not the other way around."

Tapping Sam on his shoulder, Steve beckoned on

him to follow him, and while they walked, told him to learn from that.

Sam stepped behind the teacher, and as they walked back to the school in silence, he thought *what a wonder the ant is!*

The teenager has a lot to learn about finance and needs to learn from the ant. So, we can succeed financially, there is a lot to learn for us all, about the tiny winy creatures:

MONEY ON ERRAND

Children can be taught at a young age that money is not real, but their way to get the things they want in life, like a messenger you send on an errand to get things done. If you have a busy home with ten or more little children and lots of work to be done, it might take you a long time to get things done; but if you employ one or two helpers to assist, this will be really helpful to get things done on time. So, the more helpers, the faster things get done. Money can be like that, just a tool to use to get things done.

Money can help you to get the things you want to achieve. But you don't say because the helpers are helping you with your house chores then you fall in love with your staff and marry your employee. That is like falling in love with money or loving money. We use cash but reserve our love for God and the people around us, not money. When we are faithful with money, then we get TRUE RICHES.

FAITHFULNESS WITH MONEY

True love often isn't just that, what often comes with it is the desire to have children. In order to responsibly do this, you need the right attitude to money beforehand, as not only will your finances be affected, but you need to pass on good spending habits and positive attitudes towards money to your children.

True riches include knowledge of the truth. If kids are not faithful with money, they will not know how to be faithful with all other important riches: loving people, discovering one's mission in life, and living to pursue the purpose why one was created.

True riches are channelled to us when we care for people, are kind to people, putting the priority of love forward, and knowing how to be faithful in things. Kids must be faithful first in worldly riches: money. They must have the right attitude towards money first. If they are not faithful with money, they cannot be faithful in other matters.

Every employer is looking for hardworking people, skillful people, who must have been tested and proven in one way or another, including money. Kids must be prepared to be faithful in all matters regarding money.

THE HISTORY OF MONEY

The first thing you need to do in order to teach your kid about money is to explain the history of money. Tell them about how people used to trade with their neighbours: "I will give you apples and you will give me carrots" kind of transactions. Then they realised that some things take longer to grow, so they decided that some things are worth more. This evolved when they came to the market to trade for the things they wanted.

The idea of money came about when people weighed pieces of gold or silver and and traded them by weight (think of the British currency, the "Pound", or the Israeli currency, "Shekel", which means "something that is weighed"). Explain to your young kid that money was a great thing that happened to us because we can buy whatever we want and not just what our neighbours grow.

THINGS TO NOTE

1. POCKET MONEY

Pocket money can often be the answer to many behavioural issues parents experience with their children [13]. Explain Pocket money – given weekly, say, in return for jobs around the house. Decide if you want to give your kids pocket money every week or as a reward for doing chores. Stick to at least once a week, because young kids' perception of time is not fully developed, and seven days seems to them like a very long time.

Some parents believe that giving pocket money should not be a reward. Others think that it is a good way to teach kids that money does not just fall from the sky and that we need to work for it. If you have difficulties finding chores for young kids, remember that small things like making the bed, helping clear the table after dinner and helping with the laundry can be fun chores that will teach children responsibility and sharing. Whatever you choose, stick to your schedule and always, hold a ceremony of giving your kids their resource.

2. EMOTIONAL CHORES

If you do choose to give money based on chores, remember you do not have to reward your kids for things they do for you. You can always reward them for things they do for themselves. "Emotional stretches" are a good reason to reward young kids (even older kids, teens and adults).

Give them coins each time they manage to do something that was hard for them. Being nice to a sibling, doing their homework without being told, taking a shower by themselves, waiting patiently when mum or dad are on the phone. Every time they do something that is hard for them, reward them to promote their good behaviour and personal growth.

3. POCKET MONEY RULES

When you choose to give pocket money as a reward, remember that the rules must be understood by everyone involved. Kids must understand how much you give and for what. If your child can read, make a list of the chores (and emotional stretches) with their matching reward amount. If your child is younger, draw pictures or cut them from a magazine and draw circles to represent the coins they will get for each task. Having an understanding will prevent bargaining, and allow both parents to handle the situation in the same way.

4. MONEY MANAGEMENT

Kids must know what falls into the category of what they need to purchase and what comes out of mum and dad's budget. Think about this before you start teaching your kid about money. You must be clear with yourself whether you pay for food, for snacks at school, for sweets, for treats or for anything else the kids ask for. Whatever you decide is good, as long as you have a good explanation for yourself and you stick to it.

5. PIGGY BANK

Get your child a box to put their money in. Any piggy bank that does not allow the kids to take the money out is a cruel thing for your kid. It does the exact opposite of what money management is all about. Money is not there to keep. It is there to use wisely.

A piggy bank is a good way to teach your child mathematics and the importance of saving. With the coins in a piggy bank, you can teach your child counting, subtraction or addition. If you are using a piggy bank to teach younger children math, make sure to count the coin loudly as they drop in the till. Older children can learn addition by adding up the money they have collected. They can also learn subtraction by removing a certain amount from the money to buy something.

Today, online banking applications are available in which you can set up a digital 'savings pot' for your children. If you approach this with the right attitude with your children, you can make this into a fun activity.

Allow them to monitor their 'savings pot' with your supervision. Allow them to check it each week and motivate them to keep adding to it.

By making this into a fun activity, you are encouraging your children to have a 'bigger picture' mindset.

6. LESS IS SOMETIMES MORE

Young kids find it hard to understand that a £1/ $1 coin is worth more than 20 coins of 5 pence/5 cents each. It takes a while for them to understand that the value of the money is not measured by the number of coins. Therefore, always use the smallest coins to give them money, to give them the feeling they have plenty of money.

Around the age of 6, when they learn the arithmetic of money at school, they will learn the value of each coin. When they do understand this, start exchanging single pence/cents for 10 pence/10 cents, 10 pence/cents for 25 or 50 pence/cents, and 50 pence/cents for pounds/dollars, etc.

7. WALLET

Get your kid a wallet to take with them whenever you go out. When a young kid takes a wallet with them for shopping, this is the greatest lesson about money management. When you go shopping and your kid asks for you to buy them things, refer them to their wallet and explain what they can buy with the money that they have.

Always show them the options, "This costs this many coins, another thing you want costs that many coins," and teach them to choose. When they see the money going out of their own wallet, they are not so enthusiastic about buying things, and if they are still enthusiastic, the feeling disappears after the first time when they realise they have no money left in their wallet.

8. LOANS

If you go with your kid somewhere and they did not bring their wallet, use the opportunity to teach them about lending and let them borrow some money until you get home. Only lend them amounts they can return and make sure they give you the money back the minute you get home.

If they have their wallet with them but not enough money, and they ask for an allowance, make sure they understand what this means. Again, time is not something they understandand if you tell them, "That means that next month I will not give you your pocket money." They might not understand.

Just like in real life, teach them that things that require loans also require more time to think about. In these cases, not giving them the loan, or giving part of the loan is better for your kids than being nice and giving it to them whenever they want.

9. SAVINGS

The first time your young children ask you for a loan, be happy, because now you can teach them about savings. See, it's only when they begin to truly interact with money and develop a desire for it, that you should approach the subject. Only when kids want something beyond their financial means can you explain why saving money is a good idea. Teach them to always put at least 10% of their money aside. 10%, though it doesn't sound like much, is a consistent rate of saving that is healthier long-term than saving huge amounts sporadically. It's also better than dedicating an exact financial number, like £100 per month, as it means the number you save will increase in line with inflation.

At a young age, they will not understand what 10% is, but tell them that it is a tiny piggy bank in the piggy bank of money you keep there for emergency. Alternatively, you can use the digital 'savings pot' we talked about earlier too (this will have a similar effect, and may just scratch their digital itch for using technology). The 10% you save will be the money you keep for something big or special that you want later. Tell them to put one out of every ten coins in the tiny piggy bank. Saving is a good lesson in waiting, something that is hard for young kids because their perception of time is not fully formed.

Right behind the subject of birds and bees is talking to kids about money; and money is one of the most difficult conversations for parents. Deciding what to tell them about earning, savings and growing cash can be a difficult task, mainly since many of us were never given money management skills at home and perhaps still do not know a whole lot about the subject in thefirst place.

This book provides you with a framework to discuss money with your kids, and will help you establish a foundation to share your values about finance with them. The current economic and credit crisis is, at the very least, anecdotal evidence that our views on money need some improvement, especially if we hope our children will not repeat our mistakes and will, therefore, become good earners, savers and stewards of their own resources.

A recent survey among secondary/high school and university students revealed kids pick up their views and values about money and finances at home, largely through observation and by hearing their parents talk about money. In other words, whether we intentionally teach them or not, our kids will learn the good and the bad we have to offer regarding financial matters.

Clearly, it would be a great step for us to make this process more deliberate and ensure the way we see money, and what we teach our children about it help them in the long run.

THE NEW METAPHOR

Money is energy. This is a metaphor we need to understand and communicate to our kids. We live in great countries where many people have started with nothing and have built up amazing fortunes. Many others have lost it all overnight due to corporate failures, fraud or poor judgment.

For some others, however, money is what keeps a roof over the heads, gives comfort, or even keeps up at night if they do not have what they need. For these reasons, money is typically a very emotional subject. For some, money is insecurity, pain and shame. For others, money is pride, greed, fun and excitement.

None of these emotions are ultimately healthy when they are attached to the way we see money. And whether we like it or not, we tend to pass on these emotionally charged views on money as part of our values to our children during their upbringing.

Would you like to see your children grow in gup, afraid of money, or having an unhealthy attachment to what money represents in terms of material things or immediate gratification? My guess is you probably would not. This is why we need a different metaphor when we discuss money. It is nothing to be feared or pursued obsessively.

Money is just energy. Energy is neutral and is all around us in the physical world. The cash and the credit/debit cards we keep in our pockets are just expressions of money. Imagine that you need four pints of milk. Getting it is really simple: you reach into your pocket and use a few pounds/dollars to buy your milk at the store. But what would happen if you could not get anyone to sell you milk in exchange for your money? You would have to put in a lot of hard work to obtain it, perhaps driving to a distant dairy farm or raising a cow yourself! That would certainly take a lot of valuable time and energy from you.

In modern times, we do not have to take such drastic measures to procure a measly four pints of milk. We have figured out that it is far more efficient for each of us to specialise in our own functions (jobs) and trade units of energy (cash) in exchange for our labour and for what we need (food and shelter). This is a simple formula that works to optimize the flow and use of energy of our society. Meaning, the farmer who has the milk sells it to the supermarket, then the supermarket sells the milk to us - we all have different jobs/functions in the process. In other words, money is energy; and we get to have an amount that is proportional to how much of energy we give out to the world.

THE PROPERTIES OF ENERGY AND MONEY

Any science book will tell you that energy has four key properties: it can be transferred, it can take multiple forms, it can be only converted from one form to another, and because of that, it can never be created or destroyed.

If you think about it, money has much in common with energy, as it can be transferred and it can be converted into many forms. Now, can money be created or destroyed? Technically, yes. You could take all your cash and burn it in the living room fireplace, but this is not the right way to think about it. A more logical approach to the indestructibility of money is as follows:

Imagine you are a frontiers man or woman and you arrive to the vast plains of Montana in the 1800s. Through much labour and hard work, you convert a big expanse of land into a productive farm and as a result, you emerge as a wealthy land owner and farmer. You did not destroy the land, you transformed it. Before you arrived, the energy of that land was serving nature and the animals of the region. Now it belongs to you and you can turn its bounty into cash and become a rich person. You took the energy of your work and the gift of nature and transformed them into a cash machine.

We can come up with many other examples, including inventions and new ways of doing business (such as the Internet), but I think you get the point. Energy and money are very close relatives!

What you do with the two and how you make them apply to your life is what really matters. The possibilities are truly endless.

THE EDUCATIONAL VALUE

There is educational value of seeing money as energy. One of the most important milestones in the mental development of children is when they finally make an unequivocal connection between cause and effect in the key areas of their life. Some popular examples include: if they touch fire they get burned; if they do not finish their homework, they get a terrible grade; if they are helpful around the house, they score a nice allowance.

Money is a subject that requires cause and effect thinking in order to be understood and mastered. What is most important for kids and young people to grasp is that behaviour has a direct impact on a person's ability to accumulate wealth. There is nothing mysterious about it; it is cause and effect in action. In other words, there are certain skills and actions that attract more money to us (saving, budgeting, investing, etc.), and there are others that push money away from us (overspending, abusing credit cards, etc.). It is that simple.

In today's society, where social media and other such digital marketing strategies are constantly in your face when you use internet-enabled digital devices - it can be difficult to avoid those aspects of technology that distract you from positive spending and saving.

To illustrate this point, here are some common statements children hear about money. The way these statements are presented is based on emotion and not on logical or cause-and-effect thinking. These emotionally charged statements diminish your children's ability to think about money logically and are likely to seed in them negative beliefs about wealth, which could seriously affect them in the future. See if you can spot the logical flaws before reading the explanation:

1. "That family has money, we don't."

This is something we previously mentioned earlier in the book, and is likely going to be something you will hear at least a few times throughout your child's years, particularly as a teenager. While it is probably true that a particular family is presently wealthier than your own, a statement like this presents a relative condition (they have more than us right now) as absolute and unchangeable. To the impressionable mind of a child, it may sound as a permanent reality and imply he comes from a family cursed with misfortune.

It is far better and more productive to avoid comparisons with other people and establish that your current situation can be changed. Focus on discussing possible actions that can improve the conditions of the family, such as avoiding unnecessary expenses, reading books about investing, brainstorming business ideas, etc.

2. "If you want to have money, you have to work hard."

Money, how you choose to earn it and and how much you earn is not necessarily determined by skill, talent or even drive. Therefore, this statement is only partially true, and is therefore extremely deceptive. Hard work can produce financial rewards and many wealthy people worked very hard to build and preserve their fortune. However, hard work is another absolute view that negates other possibilities. For example, there are many people who worked hard to find the right opportunity, but did not have to struggle so much once they positioned themselves properly.

This is how many fortunes in the Internet were created. Others were lost because some people put their heads down and worked hard without looking out for changes in the horizon. Hard work alone does not create wealth. It is only through a combination of smart work and hard work that we can succeed. Each one of them alone is not enough; you need both.

Most kids don't work hard because they do not see dignity in labour. Ben was a 17-year-old boy who looked for summer holiday job. When he could not find any, his father advised him to go and help out in his uncle's office. But he refused, because the organization was not going to pay him. He told his friend about that in a jesting manner, but his friend Alex went for the job while he sat at home eating.

Alex did the work from 9am to 5pm everyday, without pay; yet he liked the dignity of working; a wage or salary was not his motivation. His motivation was that the experience will add growth to him; he would gain new knowledge, a working knowledge of the trade which he did.

Many years after his graduation when a lot of people were being laid off work, Alex was such a treasure to his employer because of his attitude to work that he could not be laid off; rather, he had an increase in his contract.

3. "You need money to make money."

This is a statement that is probably responsible for stalling the dreams of many people around the world. It is technically true, but is deceptive as well. The technicality is that you need investment funds to launch a new business, but the funds do not necessarily have to come from you; they can come from investors.

If the creator of a new great business idea does not have the money, there are ways to obtain it. There are countless examples of people with creative ability who started a business with an idea, and managed to convince others to invest in them, give them free advertising, etc. Today, there is a multi-billion dollar industry of venture capitalists who pour billions every year, regardless of what the economy is doing, into new business ventures that have potential. Many fail, but they only need a few to succeed to make it worth their while.

If you teach your kids that a good idea is worth a fortune (instead of telling them the statement above), you will free them to think, meditate, conceive and create. Actually, I would like to offer you a better statement: "You need salesmanship to make money." This is a lot more accurate in the world of business.

Many good ideas go nowhere because the creator does not know how to convince others on the merits of his or her creation. The good news is salesmanship is a learnable skill. Make your kids aware of the importance of a good, persuasive and polished presentation and you may be opening for them the golden doors of success.

The truth of the matter is that in the modern digital

age of today, you can get your ideas recognised much easier and cheaper - not only via marketing them on social media but in terms of actually financing your idea.

Crowdfunding campaigns have proved very popular and largely successful over the last ten years and can give you that crucial first step onto the business ladder. Working by encouraging visitors of your page to pledge their hard-earned money to your cause (your business idea). How do you do this? By giving people different rewards, depending on how much money they choose to pledge.

So, there you have it, you don't need money to make money - you can rely on the community of the internet, accessible to people across the world, to fund your project and help with your journey to success.

4. "Rich people are rarely happy."

For a start, poor people are rarely happy as well. In fact, human beings are seldom happy. Many articles online will tell you only rich people are unhappy, or at least give you the many reasons why they usually aren't happy [14]. Happiness is an emotional skill that is not connected to money in anyway. It has to do with our ability to manage our emotions and be well adjusted to our environment. There are many books written on the subject of happiness and how to obtain it. But, trust me, money is a very small factor.

Unless we are talking about dying of an untreated disease or starvation, money is not going to put a durable smile on your face. What it will do is give you more choices, offer you interesting experiences, get you peace of mind regarding your bills and, hopefully, give you a chance to contribute to charitable causes.

Do not look for happiness in money; instead, accept that you like money and teach your children that it is okay to want to have money and the opportunities it provides. Do not deny the practical benefits of having money just because it can not give you happiness. Money and happiness are simply not connected. If you want more happiness and joy, get to know yourself from your creator's perspective, work hard on your personal growth of knowing this, and teach your kids to do the same.

Love God, and that went with love for people, was the main desire for Joyce, a 16-year-old girl; and this was the reason why she looked for a job in T-Mobile and she sent all her money to a Charity. She did so to free herself from the love of money.

She had been equipped with the richness of knowledge about money such that money does not make her happy or sad; money is not in control of her. She had been so trained that money does not change her mood; it does not make her happy or sad. Money does not determine her goals or happiness, it does not determine her time either, as she works part time and it does not determine how much she spends with her family or at work.

5. "I have no idea how to make or grow my money."

I could not agree with this more! You do not know before you know. What I mean is that this is something you need to learn. It is not in our genes and it is not intuitive. Becoming a savvy saver, investor, etc is not automatic. These are skills that take time to master. But do not get discouraged by that. Instead, get used to saying that you do not know it yet, but you will eventually if you learn.

Many worthwhile skills take a lifetime to master. Think about parenthood, for example. We do not come into this world with a clear idea of what it is like to be parents, but we learn. Trial and error or getting some coaching on the subject can help. We read books about parenting or even books such as this one.

But wait, maybe you could do the same with financial skills. Just realise it is a learnable skill and that a lot of progress can be made through reading or by finding a practical person (mentor). The sooner you start, the better. Introduce your child to someone who does well with money, or give them a book about financial literacy and you will probably change their lives forever.

Put your plan to teach your kids about money in action. Remember this, and whether you consciously teach your kids about money or not, they are picking up your beliefs and values on this subject already; so why not take charge of the process? Take the following simple steps and see how they work for you:

- Read this part or chapter a couple of times until you get the principles in it.
- Think about the beliefs you picked up from your own parents growing up.

- Decide which of these beliefs are helpful to build a financially free future.
- Choose the beliefs you like and let go of those that are not helpful.
- Have a conversation with your kids about money and share your values with them.
- Offer them a good book and help them find a good mentor. If you can be the mentor, even better.

FINANCIAL TIPS FOR KIDS

Here is the title of this book, and offers us a good reason to look more closely into it. So far, the point has been made that kids need financial intelligence to give them a proper headstart about money as a tool everyone needs to have a good well-being in this life.

An undeniable truth today is that although teenagers everywhere are faced with so many new learning experiences, yet one of the most important aspects of their adult life (personal finance) is not adequately covered for most kids prior to their secondary/high school graduation.

In today's hi-tech, hi-test, supercharged video game era, it's difficult to get kids' attention long enough to get them to clean their rooms, not to mention learn something about finances.

CREATIVE WAYS TO TALK ABOUT MONEY

After many bouts of trial and error, below are Financial Tips to teach kids, and a few creative ways to get their attention while doing so.

1. BANKING

Open a savings account for your child at birth and start developing your lesson plan for teaching money matters. During their teenage years open a bank account, but do not give them full reign on this account. Start by teaching the basics of deposits and withdrawals, using cheques and deposit slips. Teach them how to reconcile the account, noting that the balance on the online system may not be their actual balance.

Add a debit card when appropriate, but be very careful with this part of the lesson. It can be very costly if kids get carried away with the flow of cash from a cash machine/ online transactions that are not tracked properly.

2. TALK ABOUT MONEY MATTERS

Years ago, it was considered taboo to discuss your personal finances with your kids. In today's financial times, it is imperative that you discuss the basics and more. Making your kids comfortable with the topic starts with you getting comfortable discussing money matters first.

Start with basic conversations about savings, budgeting and banking. Use your real life experiences such as bank fees that you notice on your bank statement. Share your strategy on how you plan to reduce or eliminate those fees going forward. You'll be surprised how much children engage when you start including them in what used to be considered a "grown ups only" discussion.

3. BASIC BUDGETING

Start teaching kids basic budgeting skills early; and as they grow, progressively increase the lessons to the point of developing their own budget. Basic money management requires that you track your spending and identify where your funds are going. This is one of the biggest tips you will teach your children. This is a simple process that once it becomes a habit it will prove to be very beneficial to them over time.

4. NEEDS VS. WANTS

Making a difference between needs and wants to a child can be challenging because teenagers think everything they want is a need. Help them identify the basics of food, shelter and clothing (not the latest fashion). Although they may be able to get an item that they want but don't necessarily need, make sure they understand that it should be included in their budget in order for them to make the purchase.

Modern digital marketing strategies often blur the lines between what 'want' and 'need' really mean, bombarding you with sponsored posts on Instagram and 'suggested for you' marketing on Facebook - there truly is no escape. You have quite the challenge on your hands in tackling the blurred lines between social media and other such digital marketing and the importance of saving your money for what you need/savings towards something bigger and more important.

5. CREDIT CARD

Teach your kids that credit should NOT be used; but where it has to be used, it has to be with care. Help them understand how buying something they want (but don't necessarily need) on credit now could result in acquiring too much debt, leading to problems later. Use the credit card statement as a teaching tool to share the concept of simple versus compound interest.

Show your teens that only about 15% of each minimum payment goes toward the principal balance and the remaining 85% goes towards interest. They need to understand that a £3,000/$3,000 balance could take close to 40 years to pay off if they pay the minimum payment each month.

6. UNDERSTANDING CREDIT SCORES

Most people, not to mention teenagers, are clueless about credit scores and how to establish and maintain good credit. Credit scores reflect how well you manage your credit. The scores are similar to the grades that students receive in school. Teach your children the types of credit relationships to establish and maintain, primarily with banks. Encourage them to always strive for A credit by paying their bills on time and not obtaining too much credit.

7. INVEST NOW

Investing is a tool that can be taught early. Teach your

teens that people have ownership in various companies such as British Petroleum, Amazon, Microsoft, Apple, Walmart, Xerox and the local cable stations. They can also have ownership in these companies by purchasing stock. As an assignment, have them research different companies or industries of interest.

Have them investigate various investment options like mutual funds, stocks and bonds that might allow them to gain ownership into some of their favorite industries or companies. Now make monthly investments that should prove to be rewarding by the time they reach their thirties.

8. SECURING VALUABLES

Teach your teens that their identity is just as valuable as the items or cash that they try to safeguard and protect. By now, they may be in a position to complete applications or forms that require their social security number.

Explain the importance of not sharing their social security number, account numbers or personal identification numbers with others. Sometimes kids think that sharing this information with their best friend is okay. Explain that this is not negotiable.

Identity theft is prevalent in today's society and they don't want to become a victim.

9. KEEP IT INTERESTING

To help keep your teaching moments interesting, consider playing games like Monopoly which teaches the advantages of owning property; this shows them how their assets will start to work for them. While you're at it, teach your teens how to make changes without depending on a cash register or calculator.

10. GET ALLOWANCE, PAY YOUR OWN WAY

Have you ever noticed how fast kids can spend your money? They really do believe that your finances or endless, or that you're somehow rich just because you have a job and they don't.

Give your kids the responsibility of paying their own way and watch the spending decline. Allow them to earn an allowance that require them to be responsible for a bill such as their mobile/cell phone or weekly dinner/lunch money. Make sure you enforce the budgeting process to ensure they understand their role. You will be amazed how those spending habits change when the money comes from their wallet.

In today's society, your child may have a Spotify subscription, so you could suggest that they pay for this with the money they earn.

As adults we all want the best for our children. Ensuring that they are prepared for life is one of our most prominent roles as parents. Planning to spend as much quality time as possible on finance will interest teens. These ten exercises will give more opportunities to spend quality time teaching finance as one of life's lessons.

DAMIEN

Damien's parents took this advice and ran with it, giving Damien more financial responsibility in order to improve his work ethic and teach him the value of money.

Damien had a real passion for gaming and would spend much of his leisure time on his Xbox. Of course, as you likely know, playing against people in multiplayer games such as Call of Duty, Fortnite and Halo, unfortunately costs a significant subscription price. Priced at around £6 per month or £40 per year, this is a significant cost for any parent, but Damien's parents ensured the cost was covered - teaching Damien valuable life lessons in the process.

For a year's subscription, Damien had agreed to do one important/large-scale job around the house per week. If he didn't do the job, the Xbox would be confiscated for the following week.

Knowing the rules, Damien knew not to step out of line and was driven to keep his Xbox Live subscription, so would always keep up to his weekly tasks.

HOW TO BE SUCCESSFUL CHILDREN

This Chapter title puts the onus and responsibility of becoming financially independent on the child to make himself or herself successful. That's as it gets to be at the end of the day. But parents share that responsibility in the immediate present time. We are to set our children on the path of that successful life.

What you say and do about money has a profound influence on your child. There are money moments every day that you can use to teach your children essential skills and lessons about life. But what to say or do isn't always obvious.

Is it a good idea to pay for chores or grades? How do you help your child develop a work ethic? How do you structure an allowance to help your child learn to make choices? Why is involving your children in charity so important?

EIGHT BEHAVIOURS OF SUCCESSFUL PEOPLE

There are eight crucial behaviors that will help parents raise financially responsible children:

1. ENCOURAGE A WORK ETHIC

Work ethic is a learned behaviour, and parents are the best models to teach kids to acquire it. If you want your children to work hard and derive meaning and satisfaction from what they do, make sure you are modeling the right messages. Insisting your kids do their homework and help around the house does not guarantee they will grow up with a sense of accountability and a desire to achieve. But get them to work. Work is good!

2. GET YOUR OWN MONEY STORIES STRAIGHT

Because you send your children messages about money all the time, it is imperative that both you and your spouse are on the same page when it comes to your money stories.

A money story is an open, honest and personal story of your relationship with financial issues, especially as you grew up, because most people's relationship with money developed during childhood. You need to identify why you feel the way you do about money so you can send coherent and consistent messages to your kids.

When both parents focus on their money stories, children receive positive messages. Getting your money stories straight does not just mean that you agree on basic issues such as allowances and university savings. It also means that both of you have agreed to identify certain basic money values you want to teach your children, such as giving is good, working hard has its reward, and you don't always get everything you want.

3. FACILITATE FINANCIAL REFLECTION

As with most decisions kids make, when it comes to money decisions, they are frequently impulsive. As a financially intelligent parent, you want to teach your children how to think in terms of choices, alternatives and consequences. This is called reflective thinking.

Learning how to reflect both before and after making a decision is a great life skill, and one that is the hallmark of people who make good choices in everything from careers to relationships to investments. Financially intelligent parents teach their children to evaluate financial consequences based on available choices rather than making impulsive decisions. As a result, children recognise that there are many options available and they acquire the skill to make good choices.

4. BECOME A CHARITABLE FAMILY

By teaching your children that they can do more with money than spend it on themselves, you encourage them to become more compassionate and caring. By participating as a family in volunteer and community activities, you help your children develop empathy and a sense of responsibility to others.

Your children will realise that they have the power to make life better for others. Because children learn through modeling behaviour, you have to do more than write a cheque to charity. You need to show your children what it means to help others. Modeling charitable behaviors, including volunteerism, can jumpstart your child's empathy and desire to help others.

Today, finding the right charitable organisation to support is easier than ever. The internet is a fantastic resource in learning about all the possible organisations out there that you could choose to pledge money to. Not only do most organisations have websites, but they also have public-access documents, readily-available for you to read. Ten to twenty years ago, this wouldn't have been information that you were privy to, but now it's open season on information. You have a vast library of knowledge available at your fingertips, thanks to your digital devices.

5. TEACH FINANCIAL LITERACY

Although it is crucial to teach children how to balance a chequebook and create a budget, to become truly financially literate your children must learn within a context of values and money behaviors. Your children need a combination of concrete examples, their own experiences and financial reflection. If they do not learn to behave responsibly with money as kids, they will have to learn as adults when the cost is much higher.

One of the best tools to teach your children financial literacy is an allowance. Approaching allowances in a consistently constructive way allows you to instil decision-making wisdom in your children, rather than controlling them. An allowance also helps your children gain a well-balanced perspective about money, encouraging saving, investing and giving, in addition to spending.

6. AWARENESS OF THE VALUES YOU MODEL

Your children are tuned in to your purchasing decisions. The ways you spend your money sends messages to your children about your values and life priorities. Children also notice how you spend your time; and your actions can unintentionally send messages you did not intend your children to receive.

When you miss opportunities to spend time with your children in order to put in extra hours at work, or manage your money, you are sending a message that money is more important than family. Financially intelligent parents are highly conscious of their spending habits, as well as how they balance their work and family time, and the values they communicate.

7. MODERATE EXTREME MONEY TENDENCIES

Extreme money tendencies can evolve into money disorders which cause chaos within your family, and send the wrong messages to your children.

There are several types of money disorders, ranging from excessive shopping to racking up credit card debt, to excessive frugality. Regardless of the disorder, extreme money tendencies cause your children to experience confusion and insecurity in their lives. Financially intelligent parents learn to recognise and moderate extreme money behaviours.

You also need to take into account the possibility that extreme money tendencies may just be a symptom of severe depression. Take a look at your child (or anybody in your life with money troubles) and assess their situation. Ask yourself if they are spending unhealthy durations of time on digital devices. Ask yourself if they go out and see their friends often enough. If you suspect there is an issue, always encourage them to speak to a medical professional.

8. TALKING ABOUT THE TOUGH TOPICS

Parents avoid talking about financial topics that make them uncomfortable or that seem too complicated. Although you model good money behaviours in certain ways, unless you compliment these behaviours with good money conversations, you are not going to be as effective as you should be.

Financially intelligent parents recognise teachable times each day that give you and your children the opportunity to talk about financial issues. You should welcome these opportunities, as difficult as they are, to discuss and reflect on financial decisions.

TONY

Tony, from Goole, UK, is a parent who experienced first-hand just how uncomfortable it can be to approach the difficult subjects with children.

He noticed that as his son got a part-time job (when he turned 17), his spending became more frivolous than ever before. This was likely due to the fact that he had never really been given any kind of financial freedom or responsibility, but nevertheless, the way he was spending money was unhealthy.

Tony approached the subject with his son, but with a

heavy heart. He told him a story of how he had a really good job when he was younger.

"I worked for a really high-profile tech company when I was in my twenties. I thought I was set for life, they had very big plans and we all thought they were going to take over the world." Tony explained.

"I never really saved anything because I always thought I'd continue to rise through the ranks there, I thought I was safe. Then, the next thing I knew, I was turning up to work one morning and the offices were boarded up. The owners had sold up to an even bigger firm, and we were all made redundant, effective immediately".

Tony really hammered home the point that just because you have a job and you're earning money, it doesn't mean you always will. You should save while things are good.

WHAT YOUR KIDS SHOULD KNOW

Most people learn about finance the hard way through mistakes made from practical experience. People usually aren't taught about personal finance in school. Moreover, parents don't teach their children the basics either because they don't understand it themselves, or they don't take the time to do it. So, most of us learn about money as we go through life. We make purchases, go into debt, and end up with a meagre resignation account.

BASIC FINANCIAL PRINCIPLES

What if they had made better financial decisions earlier in their life? Perhaps if they were told about some basic financial principles, they would be in a better position? Here are some basic financial principles that your kids should know to avoid making simple mistakes:

1. DON'T SPEND BEYOND YOUR MEANS.

This is such a basic principle that it would not seem to be worth mentioning; however, it is the key principle to financial success. Most financial advisors will tell you to pay yourself first by saving 6-10% of your income. You can only do that if you spend less than you make. So the first and perhaps most important rule of financial success is not to spend beyond your means.

2. SAVE FOR A RAINY DAY.

As we talked about in Tony's case, this is a particularly important point and one that children need to be aware of - despite it potentially scaring them. As soon as you start working, open a savings account as an emergency fund, a rainy day fund. A rule of thumb is to have a reserve equivalent to six month's salary in case you are out of work and (for investment).

If you have an emergency, like a major car repair or medical bill, you would need to replenish the fund if you pay your bills using your emergency savings account.

3. TEACH YOUR CHILDREN TO BE GENEROUS AND SERVE OTHERS.

How can your children serve others? Children can serve others by volunteering, helping the family, helping their friends and making a difference in society. Children who serve others feel as if they have a meaningful life, and this makes them happy. Another thing that makes children happy is generosity. Children are happy when they can help others. So, motivate your children to serve others and be generous.

I told the story of Kelly in my book *101 Tips for Child Development*. Kelly and his father went shopping in the supermarket. At the mall, Kelly met a young boy about his age crying. Kelly's dad asked of his parent. The small boy pointed to a short middle-aged man talking to the cashier. Then, Kelly's dad asked why he was crying. He said his father promised to buy him a wristwatch if he had good grades in his exam and he did. When they got to the supermarket, he knew his father does not have the money to buy him a wristwatch.

Kelly, without thinking twice, removed the wristwatch his mum got him for his eleventh birthday which he celebrated the past month and stretched it to the boy. The boy looked at Kelly, then at the wristwatch, but did not take it.

"Don't you like it?" Kelly asked.

"Yes, I do, but it's yours."

"Don't worry, you can have it."

"Really? Are you serious?"

"Yes, please. I have another one at home."

The boy then took the wristwatch happily, and ran to his father. Both father and son came to Kelly and his father. The boy's father, almost in tears, thanked Kelly and his father. The boy and his father left the supermarket happily.

"Why did you do that?" Kelly's dad asked him as soon as the boy and his dad left.

"Nothing, I just felt that I needed to help the boy, plus my teacher taught me from John 13:29 that Jesus used money for only two things, one was to buy what he needed and two was to help the needy.

He was crying and I couldn't bear that," Kelly said unflinchingly.

I can imagine the excitement on Kelly's dad's face; but at the same time, I have the instinct that Kelly learnt that from his parents.

Over time, by setting positive, giving examples for children, parents can help mould their young adult into well-rounded individuals. Just like in this scenario, I bet that you will be surprised just how much your child has been learning just from watching you.

12

HOW TO RAISE KIDS SUCCEESFULLY

If you have read *101 Tips for Child Development,* then you probably know how passionate I am about raising kids the right way. I believe that how a person is in adulthood is largely influenced by how he or she was raised as a kid.

When kids do not get positive feedback and a nurturing environment from at least one parent, the tendency is to seek acceptance and attention somewhere else – oftentimes it's through peers. Then when they become out of control, teens will think it's normal process that they go through, and going through teens is the most challenging part because it is at this stage that they are in between childhood and adulthood and on the path of finding their identity.

PROCEDURES FOR SUCCESSFUL PARENTING

Successful parenting can be achieved by all; and no matter what the situation is, it can be corrected. Here are some sound words that can help you achieve this:

1. GIVE UNCONDITIONAL LOVE AND POSITIVE ATTENTION

Love your children just for being your kids, not because they excelled in school or sports, not just because they show talent, but just for being your kids. Give them ample attention. Communicate a lot. Give hugs or reassuring touches. Take time to listen to them. Attend school functions. Enjoy activities with them. Do things together, whether it's a fun activity or house chores.

Kids love and seek their parents' attention – whether they get it in a positive or negative behaviour depends on what the parents reinforce. If they don't get the positive attention and acceptance from parents, they will always seek it somewhere else, and peers are their most likely recourse. Create a stronger bond with your kids and they will always gravitate towards that bond.

2. CREATE A POSITIVE ENVIRONMENT WITHIN EVERY KID

As kids grow, they need affirmation of what they are doing; it reinforces a habit or behavior. So always keep in mind to praise good work and achievement, no matter how little those successes will be – to them it can mean so much already, and this builds confidence in them. Support their interest and encourage them in what aptitude or talent you can see in your child.

Conversely, when they do something wrong or unpleasant, do not just reprimand without letting them know why, and if you have to reprimand, do it as calm as possible and in private – humiliation, especially in front of others creates low self-worth and resentment, and a possible start of a hostile behaviour. Also, NEVER compare one kid with another. Always remember that every kid is unique and has his or her own abilities or traits.

3. TEACH THEM RESPONSIBILITY

Love, but do not pamper. Even as little kids they have to learn responsibility, like putting away their toys, making their bed, setting aside time for studies, even sharing little bits of housework. This in particular does two things: you teach them responsibility, and it serves as a bonding activity as well.

Teaching kids responsibility also can be done by showing them that receiving something they want is sometimes a reward for a positive behaviour, and that in their little way they "worked" for what they received. It gives positive reinforcement and encouragement for a deed or action.

4. TEACH THEM TO BE KIND, HELPFUL AND TO APPRECIATE WHAT THEY HAVE

Kind, helpful and appreciative are likely none of the qualities you think about when you think of the modern child of the digital age. Unfortunately, social media and digital technologies, though definitely have their benefits, unfortunately create tensions and issues that wouldn't have even been a factor ten to twenty years ago. For the most part, it seems as though we're constantly giving in to children, whether it be buying them the latest technology, or dealing with an issue caused by something they've seen on digital technology. That's why it's more important than ever to go back to basics and teach the valuable qualities a person should have.

Teaching your kid to be kind and helpful creates a

gentle spirit within. Similarly, letting them appreciate whatever they have will create a positive outlook. When my kids were growing up and we saw unfortunate or unpleasant situations, I always told them how blessed they are that they were not in the same situation; but at the same time, seeing how blessed they are, they should pass it forward by kindness. The best way to show this is when they see this in you!

5. GIVE THEM THE GIFT OF INNER STRENGTH

Give your kids the gift of inner strength, to accept mistakes, rejection and failure in a constructive way. Kids need to know that it is normal to fail (and not being scolded for it!), and making mistakes is a good exercise to teach us inner strength. Adverse things happen in life sometimes, and the important thing is that one did ONE'S best, not THE best, and to learn from these mistakes instead of sulking and pondering over these mistakes.

Another significant way we can teach our kids inner strength is by not giving in to all they want. As parents we are sometimes guilty of doing this, but instant gratification every time will not build the kids' character. Rather, we are to help them realise that they cannot have everything they want. This should be explained thoughtfully.

It's worth noting that many aspects of the digital age are orientated around bringing people down.

Negativity on the internet is a plague, so teaching your child about their inner strength, money related or not, is crucial.

6. PUT MOTIVATION IN A POSITIVE PERSPECTIVE

When you encourage your kid to do things, especially in studies, teach your kid the value of doing his best, instead of negative programming – "study or you are grounded". This makes for a negative, short-term motivation, and will not teach your kid the value on his future.

7. TO A CERTAIN DEGREE, INVOLVE THEM WITH THE SITUATION AT HAND

How you handle this will depend on the kids' age — knowing the proper timing and manner how to say this is crucial. Are you having certain financial struggles? Serious problems? While these are adult problems, they can be communicated to the kid to a certain extent.

If done appropriately, it gives children a solid grasp of reality. The key here is to explain it in the least negative way possible without showing bitterness but rather acceptance and optimism.

8. LEARN TO SAY SORRY

As adults and parents, we are not infallible. Sometimes a sudden burst of anger from a parent, or a false accusation, will cause a child to feel dejected. Learn to apologise to them, as it teaches the child to be humble and do the same when wrong.

Good parenting involves a lot of love, patience and communication. The key is developing a close positive relationship with your kids. We only get one shot at raising our kids – once they grow up crooked, it becomes hard to correct. The greatest gift we can give our kids therefore is raising them with the proper values, attitude and character.

INTRODUCTION TO ENTREPRENEURSHIP

In this final chapter of this book, I want to touch on a matter I have skirted around in the preceding chapters: Entreprenuership.

A ONE-SIDED SYSTEM

Does talking to children about entrepreneurship at an early age make sense? Our school system is set up to lead our children into the workplace as employees, not employers. Now don't get me wrong, as a society we definitely need employees: police officers, firefighters, doctors, nurses, etc., but why not shine some light on entrepreneurship too?

Incorporating the principles and philosophy of success with emphasis on teamwork, community involvement, and entrepreneurship will no doubt go well with all types of learners of varying ages. Children deserve the opportunity to at least hear about what entrepreneurship is, why they may want to be entrepreneurial, when they could do this and, of course, how to be an entrepreneur.

We find that children are very responsive when talking about being resourceful on their own. As early as six years of age, children are starting to realise the importance behind making your own resources versus working for someone else. Unfortunately, not enough children in the world are being introduced to this kind of lifestyle.

STEPS TO ENTREPRENUERSHIP

Below are some great tips, in no particular order, to help you introduce your child to entrepreneurship.

1. STORY TIME

A great way to get your child started is by sharing with them inspiring stories of kids today who are already entrepreneurs. The internet is a great resource, making available great stories about kid entrepreneurs from around the world, what they are doing right now and how they are doing it.

When sharing inspiring kid entrepreneur stories, ask your children questions like, How did they do that? Why did they do it? Do you think you can do something like that? What makes you feel that way? If you get an answer like, "I can't do that," then ask a follow-up question: Well, if you could do that, how would you do it?" This usually gets a response like, "Oh!" And whatever follows that, don't forget to show your kids pictures, or watch videos or check out newsclips of kid entrepreneurs. It's also quite effective when kids hear the stories right from another kid's mouth.

2. DAY OUT/SCHOOL TRIP FUN

Contact local businesses or news agencies to see if you could arrange for your kids to visit with them and get a behind-the-scenes look at how the particular business operates. Approach businesses that hold a high-interest level for your kids. Let the places know that you are interested in a behind-the-scenes look at their business' operations for your child/children and their friends who are learning about entrepreneurship.

I highly recommend that you bring your children's friends too, so you all can enjoy the experience together so that your child has likeminded individuals to discuss their finding with.

3. FUNDRAISER

Have a fundraiser for a cause that is very important to your child or have them pick products they think they can sell either in the neighborhood or to local businesses. Let your kids bring in some of their friends that want to be a part of the action.

Have them brainstorm ideas and narrow the list down to a few that they all agree on. Assist them in organising the timing and the locations they conduct these "business meetings."

4. MAKE PLANNING FUN

Start planning with your kids. For the younger kids create a plan book from scratch, even some of the older kids can get into this too. Design it however they want. They can add stickers or make fancy title pages within their planner. The point here is for them to personalise it as much as they like.

You can even pick up an inexpensive planner for their use. Talk to them about the importance of using the planner daily, and getting into the habit of planning for each day the night before. Explain to them how this will start to free up more time for them to do the things they want to be doing, instead of just doing the things they have to be doing as they become more focused.

In addition to a planner/goal book, have the children create a journal as well, writing down brief entries into a personal journal on a daily basis of things that interest or perplex them is a great way to get them started with being responsible, planning for their future, and allowing them time for natural, real world problem solving!

5. USE YOUR IMAGINATION

Go online or to your library and search for wonderful places around the globe that you would love to visit sometime in your life. Have the kids look through books or at websites. Take notice as to what types of places intrigue them the most and talk about those places. Ask them what they would have to do in order to get to visit these wonderful places. Have them search how much it would cost to fly there if you were to leave today.

What could they do to raise enough money for a trip like that? What other expenses may they encounter planning for a trip to that location? If it's something they really want to do, have them list it in their journal as one of their goals and then start to list all the things they need to do in order to reach that goal.

6. BREAK OUT THE SEASONS

Sharpen your children's sense and general memory by playing memory games/puzzles. Play silly and fun games like "Identify that smell" or "Name that object" where children are paired off in teams and try to identify blindfolded certain odors or identify what object they are touching without being able to see it. Not only is it fun but it will also help enhance the brain performance of its participants, thereby increasing creativity and problem solving abilities, two critical ingredients in becoming an entrepreneur!

7. DON'T BE SHY

I know that there are lots of old fashioned parents out there that think that the household finances should be top secret and not o be discussed with children. When it comes to bill time or any time money needs to be discussed, don't be shy. Share with children the expenses and income you manage each month and each year. Show them the bills you pay, how much they are, and when they are due. Explain to them how you make your payments on these bills. If you write cheques to pay them, then have them help you with that. If you pay some of your bills online, have them help with that too. Don't, be shy, show them how you balance your chequebook and keep track of your finances.

If you are not sure how yourself, research it online or at the library and learn it with your children. You would be surprised as to how much kids are interested in learning how to pay bills, balance a bank account, or even create a budget. It increases their interest in math by giving them purpose for learning the subject!

8. TRY SOMETHING DIFFERENT

Have a "what I want to be when I grow up" get-together with your child and their friends; where everyone comes to the get-together as what they want to be when they grow up. Children play the role and parents encourage them by catering for the children's needs.

You can give prizes to the kids for acting their parts and encourage the role-playing. This will help them see themselves now as they could potentially become in the future, bringing the feelings of success of what it would feel like. By the parents catering for the "grown-ups" needs, the kids get the idea of what respectful/professional treatment would seem like when they actually reach their goals.

HANDS-ON KID ENTREPRENUERS

Many children across the world are venturing into entrepreneurship and making waves for themselves.

PLEASE LEAVE A 1-CLICK REVIEW!

Thank you for reading this book and engaging in the next step to establishing kids with financial management. I hope this book helped you in the same way it has helped many others.

I would really appreciate if you could take 60 seconds to write a short review for this book on Amazon, even if it's just a few sentences! Your help in spreading the word is greatly appreciated. Reviews from readers like you make a huge difference in helping new readers find helpful books like this one. I joyfully read every single review.

Just click on the link below and you will be taken straight to the review page on Amazon.

Thank you!

[Review Book Here](#)

CONCLUSION

The point I have emphasised throughout this book is that young children can learn about money from as early an age as three.

Having a healthy attitude towards money is important to help your kid grow with skills that lots of schools are not going to give them. They are going to need them desperately the minute they leave home. If you think they are too young to know about money, remember that one day they will have to pay for their expenses.

THE BOOK

This author observes how kids today are bombarded with advertising, and keep up peer pressure. She sees money management and financial skills as a must subject matter for parents to continually cover with their kids throughout their childhood and teen years. The tips to do just this are presented in this book in clear readable way for all to understand, follow and apply.

If your kids become financially responsible at an early age, chances are much greater they will continue throughout their lifetime. This is an aim this book can help you fulfil.

OTHER BOOKS YOU'LL LOVE!

CLICK ON THE BOOKS

Link to Book

162 | OTHER BOOKS YOU'LL LOVE!

Link to Book

Link to Book

Link to Book

Link to Book

164 | OTHER BOOKS YOU'LL LOVE!

Link to Book

Link to Book

OTHER BOOKS YOU'LL LOVE! | 165

Link to Book

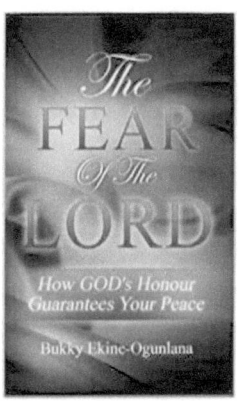

Link to Book

OTHER BOOKS YOU'LL LOVE!

Link to Book

REFERENCES

1. https://www.fnbwford.com/pdf/Talk%20to%20your%20kids%20about%20money.pdf
2. https://money.usnews.com/money/personal-finance/family-finance/articles/how-to-help-adult-children-become-financially-independent
3. https://www.ats.edu/uploads/uploads/lancaster-spending-plan-workbook.pdf
4. https://www.foolproofme.org/studentpirgs/images/Student_PIRGs_debt_trap_brochure-print.pdf
5. https://www.daveramsey.com/blog/how-to-teach-kids-about-money

6. https://www.nomoredebts.org/budgeting/budgeting-tips/smart-money-management-ideas-for-kids
7. https://masassets.blob.core.windows.net/cms/files/000/001/092/original/Difficult_Conversations_-_Talking_about_money.pdf
8. https://www.waldorflibrary.org/images/stories/articles/giftofno_mcglauflin.pdf
9. https://www.gogoshopper.com/resources/learning-the-value-of-money-lesson-plans-and-activities.html
10. https://www.practicalmoneyskills.com/assets/pdfs/lessons/lev9-12/TG_Lesson10.pdf
11. https://www.daveramsey.com/blog/stop-impulse-buys
12. https://www.sec.state.ma.us/sct/sctinv/pdf/Danger_of_Credit_Cards.pdf
13. https://www.researchgate.net/publication/4886768_Pocket_money_and_child_effort_at_school
14. https://www.theatlantic.com/family/archive/2018/12/rich-people-happy-money/577231/

www.ingramcontent.com/pod-product-compliance
Lightning Source LLC
Chambersburg PA
CBHW020034120526
44588CB00030B/278